Great Meals in Minutes was created by
Rebus, Inc.
and published by Time-Life Books.

Rebus, Inc.

Publisher: Rodney Friedman
Editor: Shirley Tomkievicz
Executive Editor: Elizabeth P. Rice
Art Director: Ronald Gross
Senior Editors: Brenda Goldberg,
Ruth A. Peltason
Food Editor and Food Stylist: Grace Young
Photographer: Steven Mays
Prop Stylist: Zazel Wilde Lovén
Associate Editor: Alexandra Greeley
Editorial Assistants: Donna Kalvarsky,
Michael Flint
Photography, Styling Assistant: Cathryn·
Schwing
Editorial Board: Angelica Cannon, Sally
Dorst, Lilyan Glusker, Kim MacArthur,
Valerie Marchant, Joan Whitman

Time-Life Books Inc.
is a wholly owned subsidiary of

Time Incorporated

Founder: Henry R. Luce 1898–1967
Editor-in-Chief: Henry Anatole Grunwald
President: J. Richard Munro
Chairman of the Board: Ralph P. Davidson
Executive Vice President: Clifford J. Grum
Editorial Director: Ralph Graves
Group Vice President, Books: Joan D. Manley

Time-Life Books Inc.

Editor: George Constable
Executive Editor: George Daniels
Director of Design: Louis Klein
Board of Editors: Dale M. Brown, Thomas A.
Lewis, Robert G. Mason, Ellen Phillips,
Gerry Schremp, Gerald Simons, Rosalind
Stubenberg, Kit van Tulleken
Director of Administration: David L. Harrison
Director of Research: Carolyn L. Sackett
Director of Photography: John Conrad Weiser

President: Reginald K. Brack Jr.
Senior Vice President: William Henry
Vice Presidents: George Artandi, Stephen L.
Bair, Peter G. Barnes, Robert A. Ellis,
Juanita T. James, Christopher T. Linen,
James L. Mercer, Joanne A. Pello,
Paul R. Stewart

Editorial Operations
Design: Anne B. Landry (art coordinator);
James J. Cox (quality control)
Research: Phyllis K. Wise (assistant director),
Louise D. Forstall
Copy Room: Diane Ullius (director),
Celia Beattie
Production: Gordon E. Buck,
Peter Inchauteguiz
Correspondent: Miriam Hsia (New York)

SERIES CONSULTANT
Margaret E. Happel is the author of *Ladies
Home Journal Adventures in Cooking,
Ladies Home Journal Handbook of Holiday
Cuisine,* and other best-selling cookbooks, as
well as the translator and adapter of Rebecca
Hsu Hiu Min's *Delights of Chinese Cooking.*
A food consultant based in New York City,
she has been director of the food department
of *Good Housekeeping* and editor of
American Home magazine.

WINE CONSULTANT
Tom Maresca combines a full-time career
teaching English literature with writing
about and consuming fine wines. He is now
at work on *The Wine Case Book,* which
explains the techniques of wine tasting.

For information about any Time-Life book,
please write:
Reader Information
Time-Life Books
541 North Fairbanks Court
Chicago, Illinois 60611

Library of Congress Cataloging in Publication Data
American regional menus.
    (Great meals in minutes)
    Includes index.
    1. Cookery, American. 2. Menus.
    3. Cooks—United States—Biography.
I. Time-Life Books. II. Series.
TX715.A5275 1984   642'.0973   83-9321
ISBN 0-86706-163-4 (lib. bdg.)
ISBN 0-86706-162-6 (retail ed.)

Cover: Susy Davidson's pork chops with
caramelized apples, acorn squash with pecans,
and braised red cabbage. See pages 52–55.

Great Meals
IN MINUTES

AMERICAN REGIONAL MENUS

TIME-LIFE BOOKS, ALEXANDRIA, VIRGINIA

Contents

Meet the Cooks

DEIRDRE DAVIS

Deirdre W. Davis received her training at Boston's Modern Gourmet professional chef's program, under the direction of Madeleine Kamman. After receiving her chef's teacher's diploma, she continued her career as a chef, cooking teacher, and administrator in Madeleine Kamman's cooking schools both in France and in the United States. Now she is the co-director of Cooking at the French Library, a cooking school in Boston, her hometown.

RAYMOND SOKOLOV

New Yorker Raymond Sokolov has written about food for *New York* magazine, *Cue, The Atlantic,* and *The New York Times,* of which he is the former food editor and critic. As the food columnist for *Natural History* magazine, he has traveled extensively across America in search of authentic regional cooking. His cookbooks include *Great Recipes from The New York Times, The Saucier's Apprentice,* and *Fading Feast.*

PATRICIA LENZ

Patricia Lenz, a native New Yorker, was an amateur cook when she opened her restaurant, A Moveable Feast, in 1970. A showcase for American foods and wines, this Long Island restaurant received the highest rating from *The New York Times* in 1976. She and her husband own a vineyard and winery on Long Island's North Fork, and she is a director of the Long Island Grape Growers Association.

SUSY DAVIDSON

Susy Davidson earned the Grand Diplome from L'Ecole de Cuisine La Varenne in Paris, where she subsequently worked as an editorial associate. While living in France, she was an assistant to Simone Beck at her Provence-based cooking school. She was Julia Child's associate chef on television's *Good Morning America* and is currently culinary director of *The Cook's Magazine,* published in Connecticut.

RICHARD NELSON

Richard Nelson, an Oregon-based cooking teacher and cookbook author, has studied food preparation with many notable American chefs, including James Beard. He was a founding member of the International Association of Cooking Schools and served as its president for two terms. Besides writing a weekly syndicated food column, he is also a cookbook author and has recently published *Richard Nelson's American Cooking*.

MIRIAM UNGERER

Miriam Ungerer is a professional journalist and self-taught cook. A native of South Carolina, she has lived and cooked in various regions of the United States. She has also explored many European cuisines—all of which have influenced her food writing and her cooking style. She has written for *The New York Times*, *Food & Wine*, and *Harper's Bazaar*. She is the author of *Good Cheap Food* and *Country Food*, a cookbook that spotlights the foods of Long Island, her home at present.

ANN SERANNE

Ann Seranne, who lives in Blairstown, New Jersey, has been cooking and writing about American food for many years. During her distinguished food career, she has been executive editor of *Gourmet* magazine and has managed her own food public relations firm. She has edited 40 cookbooks and has written over 20 of her own, including the *Complete Book of Home Preserving* and two blender cookbooks.

BEVERLY COX

Beverly Cox holds the Diplome d'Excellence from Maxim's in Paris and the Grand Diplome from the Cordon Bleu. As a food stylist, she develops recipes for clients and is Food Editor and Director of Food Styling for *The Cook's Magazine*. Now living in Connecticut, she is the author of *Gourmet Minceur* and *Minceur Italienne*, and the coauthor, with Joan Whitman, of *Cooking Techniques*.

LAURA SANDIFER

A native of New Jersey, Laura Sandifer now lives in New York. Although she is a Northerner, she specializes in Southern food. She learned these styles, as well as fine continental cooking, from her grandmother, and her parents, who ran a successful catering business. As wife of a New York State Supreme Court judge, Laura Sandifer entertains frequently, and cooking remains her favorite pastime.

American Menus in Minutes

The cuisine that Americans have inherited and developed is one of the most diverse and complex in the world. American cooking today is the product of many factors: native inventiveness, indigenous foods, immigrants' recipes, modern technology, and national pride. It is a mix that includes regional recipes together with the national standbys all Americans enjoy: steak and potatoes, hot dogs and baked beans, apple pie and ice cream.

Change has been a constant in the evolution of American cooking. The earliest settlers in Plymouth or in Jamestown often had to abandon their Old World eating habits in order to survive. They turned to the Indians, the original American cooks, who taught them how to prepare the abundant native edibles at hand: corn, beans, squash, turkeys, moose, soft-shelled crabs and large-clawed lobsters, cranberries, blueberries, beach plums, maple syrup, sweet potatoes, and sunchokes. And as pioneers traveled westward, they learned to appreciate pecans, persimmons, wild rice, peanuts, buffalo meat, a variety of wild berries, avocados, and green chilies. These adventurers encountered other unfamiliar foodstuffs that helped to change their food vocabulary: sunflower seeds, onions, hickory nuts, huckleberries, black-eyed peas, dandelions, and fiddlehead ferns.

As America attracted successive generations of immigrants, the New World's cooking continued to evolve. The newcomers brought their traditional recipes—the English, apple pie; the French, chowder; the Dutch, cookies, coleslaw, and waffles—and some European foodstuffs as well. But often they found their larders short of all the ingredients necessary to reproduce their own familiar meals, so they improvised with America's bounty and created totally new recipes. Part American, part foreign, these were assimilated into the national cooking repertoire. Eventually, creative American cooks—in rural communities and in burgeoning cities—integrated the Old and the New Worlds. The result: America's regional cooking heritage.

Boiled shrimp and lobster, some raw oysters, and fresh cuts of pork and beef, opposite, are ready for an American-style meal. On the tabletop as well is a cornucopia of fresh ingredients from American regional cooking (clockwise, from top left): zucchini, broccoli, corn, tomatoes, cabbage, eggs, acorn and butternut squash, heads of garlic, okra, potatoes, and asparagus.

Without a doubt, the greatest culinary transformation has come with nineteenth- and twentieth-century technology. Entrepreneurs in the food industry developed techniques for canning, freezing, dehydrating, pickling, or precooking—then packaging—all manner of foods. The end result is long shelf life, mass use, and, in many cases, easier cooking. How much easier is made clear by looking at a few examples. In days gone by, housewives used to corn their own beef, salt their own pork, brew the family's beer, and churn the butter. They made cottage cheese by pouring warmed soured milk into a coarse cloth bag and hanging it up for several hours to drain. They made their own gelatin by boiling down calves' hooves.

During the nineteenth century, railroads and improved roadways speedily carried fresh foods across the land and gave Americans a wider choice of foods year round. Better transportation, plus the advent of refrigerated railroad cars, helped turn Americans into a nation of confirmed beef eaters. Cattle raised in the West were transported to Chicago, where they were butchered and processed, and the meat was then shipped by road or railroad across the country. Today, sophisticated transportation networks exist, enabling speedy delivery of both fresh and frozen foods all over the nation; planes bring in a wide variety of foodstuffs from overseas.

Major kitchen appliances—refrigerators, gas and electric stoves, freezers—developed for general use in the early twentieth century have transformed eating and cooking habits. Mechanical refrigerators, which replaced in-home ice boxes chilled by blocks of pond ice, and freezers are vital for the reliable preservation of fresh foods. Without refrigerators or freezers, most perishable foods would have to be eaten where they are produced or would have to be preserved in some way—by salting or pickling, for instance—which would destroy their fresh flavor. Modern refrigeration also makes possible the creation of dishes that require chilling or freezing, such as mousses, soufflés, and ices.

Improved stoves have freed cooks from the drudgery of chopping wood for cook stoves, of stoking fires, and of guessing at oven temperatures and cooking times. Sophisticated kitchen devices—blenders, beaters, toasters, juicers, food processors—simplify and speed up food preparation.

Jet travel, television, magazines, restaurants, and cookbooks expose American cooks to a wide world of new, exciting—and often exotic—recipes. Since the end of

World War II, this country's cooking has passed with startling speed through many phases—convenience foods, international foods, gourmet foods, health foods, fast foods—back to fresh, all-American foods. Proud of their culinary heritage, Americans are adapting old-time recipes to modern kitchens and life-styles. An overriding factor in today's life-styles is lack of time. Practically everyone finds time at a premium, and along with concern for preparing nutritious, enjoyable food goes the need to put meals together quickly. This book is designed to satisfy the modern cook on both counts.

On the following pages, nine of America's most talented cooks present twenty-seven complete menus featuring American fare that can be made in an hour or less. They use fresh produce—no canned vegetables, powdered sauces, or other questionable shortcuts. The other ingredients (vinegars, spices, herbs, etc.) are all high quality yet available for the most part in supermarkets or, occasionally, in specialty shops. Each of the menus serves four people and includes side dishes that work perfectly with the main course.

The color photographs accompanying each meal show exactly how the dishes will look when you take them to the table. The cooks and the test kitchen have planned the meals for appearance as well as for taste: the vegetables are brilliant and fresh, the color combinations appetizing. The table settings feature bright colors, simple flower arrangements, and attractive, if not necessarily expensive, serving pieces. You can readily adapt your own tableware to these menus in convenient ways that will please you and your guests.

For each menu, the Editors, with advice from our wine consultant and from the cooks, suggest wines and other beverages as well as appropriate desserts to accompany the meals. And there is information on the best uses for leftovers. On each recipe page, too, you will find a range of other tips, from the best way to cook lobster to the tricks for selecting the freshest produce. All the recipes have been tested meticulously, not only for taste and appearance but also to make sure that even a relatively inexperienced cook can do them within the 60-minute time limit.

BEFORE YOU START
Great Meals in Minutes is designed for efficiency and ease. The books will work best for you when you follow these suggestions:

1. Refresh yourself on the few simple cooking techniques on the following pages. They will quickly become second nature and will help you produce professional meals in minutes.

2. Read the menus *before* you shop. Each one opens with a list of all the required ingredients. Check for those few you need to buy; most items will already be on your pantry shelf.

3. Check the equipment list on pages 16–17. A good, sharp knife or knives and pots and pans of the right shape and material are essential for making great meals in minutes. This may be the time to look critically at what you

own and to plan to pick up a few things. The right equipment can turn cooking from a necessity into a creative experience.

4. Get out everything you need before you start to cook: the lists at the beginning of each menu tell just what is required. To save steps, keep your ingredients close at hand and always put them in the same place so you can reach for them instinctively.

5. Take meat and dairy products from the refrigerator early enough for them to come to room temperature; this will cut cooking time.

6. Follow the step-by-step game plan with each menu. That way, you can be sure of having the entire meal ready to serve at the right moment.

A NOTE ON AMERICAN REGIONAL STYLES
Although rapid transportation unifies the American people and fast foods are standard fare from coast to coast, regional dishes, as served in restaurants and private homes, continue to define geographical areas in the United States. Mention the Southwest, and Tex-Mex food comes to mind; or New England, and many people think of clam chowder and lobsters. To understand regional foods, you must picture the United States divided, even subdivided, into large, somewhat overlapping areas—each area distinguished by its own climate, terrain, and indigenous foodstuffs. Regional cooking styles are influenced by those factors and have been further transformed by each ethnic group of settlers that has moved in. In some cases, as among the Pennsylvania Dutch, the Old World cooking styles still persist.

NEW ENGLAND
New England food—Yankee cooking—is as simple, practical, and straightforward as the Puritan colonists who developed it and who set the tone for America's culinary tradition. They quickly adapted to the unfamiliar foodstuffs of their new homeland and created dishes that are the foundation of many modern American meals and that are synonymous with New England cooking: baked beans, fish stews, clambakes, codfish cakes, maple syrup, Indian pudding, squash, cranberries, boiled lobsters, and apple cobblers. (Raymond Sokolov's lobster feast, page 35, Deirdre Davis's fish chowder, page 23, and Miriam Ungerer's codfish balls, pages 69–70, all come from the New England tradition.) The Puritans' first harvest festival in 1621 was the forerunner of the American Thanksgiving holiday. Their menu, however, would sound unfamiliar to today's celebrants: venison, roast duck, roast goose, clams, eels, leeks, and watercress, and, according to some sources, no turkey at all.

MID-ATLANTIC
Because so many different ethnic groups settled in New York, New Jersey, and Pennsylvania, this region became a national melting pot, where no one cooking style predominates. In general, mid-Atlantic cookery—neither as unadorned as New England food nor as sumptuous as Southern—is substantial farm fare: ham and other pork products, yeast breads and coffee cakes, bakery goods and

preserves. And the coastal areas have always relied on seafood (see Patricia Lenz's menus for some Long Island fish specialties).

Three major immigrant groups left their culinary mark on the mid-Atlantic states: the English, the Dutch, and the Germans. The Germans, or "Deutschen," were the forebears of today's Pennsylvania Dutch cooks. Of the three groups, the Germans made the most enduring contribution to America's cooking in the form of Pennsylvania Dutch food: dairy products, baked goods, hickory-smoked meats, apple butter, sauerkraut, and corn relish. Deirdre Davis's Menu 1 (pages 20–21) features Pennsylvania Dutch cooking.

Delaware and Maryland are buffer states between the South and mid-Atlantic. Northern European settlers in those two states developed what we know as Eastern Shore cooking, more Southern than Northern in character: crab cakes, beaten biscuits, batter breads, and terrapin (turtle) stew.

SOUTH

Many Americans mistakenly believe that fried chicken, country-smoked hams, hominy grits, and cornbread are the sum and substance of Southern cooking. Actually, the first Southerners—who were English, Scotch-Irish, and French—greatly influenced by the Africans and the native Indians, produced such a rich and diverse cuisine that it defies simple definition. Southern food is actually a series of cuisines within cuisines. Soul food, the earthy handiwork of black cooks, consists of such classics as barbecued spareribs, black-eyed peas boiled with a ham hock or salt pork, collard greens, game stews, pigs' feet, and a soul version of the ubiquitous Southern fried chicken. Like Chinese cooks, soul-food cooks made use of every edible morsel that came their way, but unlike the Chinese, they believed in lengthy cooking.

As a matter of fact, many so-called soul-food dishes were typical of wealthy homes. An overlapping category is plantation food—lavish, elegant meals that varied from locale to locale but that consisted of seafood dishes, chicken, barbecued meats, vegetables, and extravagant desserts. Creole cooking, inspired by French, American, Indian, Spanish, and African cuisines, flourished in Louisiana. Consisting largely of highly seasoned yet subtle and elegant seafood and vegetable dishes, it was enjoyed by wealthy Louisiana landowners. The hub of Creole cooking is New Orleans. Cajun cooking is the country cousin of Creole, but it is more pungent and peppery, befitting the rugged outdoor life of its French originators, who came from Acadia, in Canada's maritime provinces.

Despite such diversity, there are several constants in the Southern cooking tradition: pork, chicken, cornbread and hominy, biscuits, sweet potatoes, shellfish, rice, and barbecued foods.

Laura Sandifer offers three very Southern menus, Beverly Cox a Cajun shrimp stew, and Raymond Sokolov an oyster-catfish-okra menu that reflects both Carolina and Louisiana styles.

MIDWEST

The cooking of the central portion of America, including the Great Lakes states as well as the mountain and plains states, is unpretentious farm/country food and has been influenced almost equally by Southern, European-immigrant, and American Indian cooks.

As the agricultural heartland of the nation, the Midwest produces abundant produce, particularly corn. A mainstay of Midwestern diets, corn has been, and continues to be, a part of American history. The recipes in this volume bear witness to its many and varied uses: see Deirdre Davis's corn fritters (page 27) and corn sticks (page 23), Laura Sandifer's corn soup (page 99), Raymond Sokolov's corn on the cob (page 35), and page 45 for Patricia Lenz's three-bean salad with hominy (a kind of preserved corn).

Other foods typical of the Midwest include pork, poultry, and beef. In many areas cooks are also expert in preparing game, buffalo, and freshwater fish.

SOUTHWEST

Texas, New Mexico, and Arizona are famous for Tex-Mex foods: chili con carne, tacos, enchiladas, chilies rellenos, and tamale pie, for example. This flamboyant cuisine is an outgrowth of the effort to modify Mexican ingredients and recipes to suit American produce and palates. It is generally, but not always, a piquant cuisine that incorporates these ingredients: avocados, tomatoes, green chilies, lemons, papayas, mangoes, coconut milk, and such herbs as cilantro, cumin, oregano, and cinnamon. Corn shows up again as an integral part of the cooking in this area: both cornmeal and corn flour are staples of Mexican and Tex-Mex cuisines. Southwesterners also love barbecues (barbacoa in Spanish), which their ancestors learned about from the early Spanish settlers, who themselves had learned this cooking method from the Indians of the Southwest and Mexico. Southwesterners have other regional favorites as well, such as agarita jelly, mustard grape pie, piñon nuts, and garbanzo salad. Anne Seranne's first menu is an example of a modified Tex-Mex approach.

Although Texans are famous for their barbecues and Tex-Mex dishes and their ranch-style meals, they are heirs to many different cooking styles: Southern, East Coast, Midwestern, Mexican, and German. A sizable number of German immigrants settled in many Texas communities. Miriam Ungerer's mixed grill (pages 72–73) is inspired by German cooking.

WEST

California, Oregon, and Washington share a love of fresh produce and seafood. Lately California has been the nation's test kitchen, a center of culinary creativity. California cooking is a style unto itself, combining informality, unconventional methods, Oriental and Mexican influences, and locally produced wines. Southern California's mild, Mediterranean-like climate makes that area an agricultural cornucopia. As a consequence, California cooks base much of their cuisine on the use of the state's fresh, readily available produce: artichokes, avocados, figs, dates, nuts, citrus fruits, and olives.

Apples are a versatile and ubiquitous ingredient in American regional cooking, and Americans eat several million bushels of apples every year. At least 900 varieties of apple grow in the United States, but only a few dozen varieties are widely cultivated and commercially marketed. Apples are by no means interchangeable. They vary in texture, sweetness, and appearance. Some are good for cooking, others suitable only for eating raw.

You can buy apples the year round, but they are at their peak in the fall, when they have just been picked. Apples you buy after November (except Granny Smiths, which are largely imported from Australia) probably come from cold storage. They may still be of high quality, but you should look them over with particular care.

Apples are sold loose, packaged in trays, and bagged. Loose ones, which you can examine, are usually more expensive. Do not buy apples with blemishes or soft spots, signs of deterioration. Packaged apples may be a better buy, but avoid packages that hide part of the fruit. If this is your only option, check the wrapping for moisture, which can indicate decay. Try to choose your apples with a definite purpose, or recipe, in mind. When buying apples to cook, allow about one pound for three cups of raw slices. Three pounds of raw apples will make a pie.

Note: the shine on the apple is not necessarily natural. Growers often coat apples lightly with an edible wax before marketing them. You can wash or buff this off if you like.

Kinds of Apples

At supermarkets or roadside stands, these are the most popular varieties.

Cortland: Two-toned red and yellow, with snowy white, somewhat tart flesh. Bruise-resistant. Good for salads, since the flesh does not darken quickly. Cooks rapidly.

Delicious: Usually large and juicy in both the Red and Golden varieties. Sweet and flavorful, but sometimes tasteless. Good raw. Golden Delicious are also good in pies, as long as you reduce the amount of sugar.

Granny Smith: Crisp, tart, lime-green; available mainly in spring and summer. All-purpose and flavorful. Keeps its shape when cooked.

Jonathan: Fragrant, flavorful, red and yellow. Almost perfectly round. Ideal for cooking and applesauce, but a poor selection for baking whole. Does not keep well.

Macoun: Large, bright red, and all purpose. Holds up well in cooking. Similar to the McIntosh. Keeps well.

McIntosh: Red-green, aromatic, crisp, tart-sweet. Good raw, sliced into salads, and poached whole. Not a good choice for pies; the slices turn mushy.

Northern Spy or *Spy:* Large, with red-blushed, yellowish skin. Tart, crisp, very juicy. One of the best cooking apples, especially for pies. Keeps well.

Pippin or *Newton Pippin:* An old-fashioned variety, yellow or green. Tart, crisp, juicy, and all purpose. Especially good for pies.

Rhode Island Greening: A tart green cooking apple, crisp and fine grained. Good for applesauce and pies.

Rome Beauty: Large and round, often deep red with yellow, mealy flesh. Suitable for baking whole with sugar and spices. Not ideal for eating raw.

Russet or *Roxbury Russet:* Sweet but with a rough, mottled skin. All purpose. Keeps well.

Winesap: Juicy, deep red, mildly tart. A late-ripening variety prized for cider and cooking versatility.

Storing Apples

Apples bought crisp and firm should keep about two weeks. To prolong storage life, do not wash apples before storing them. Handle them gently to avoid bruising, wrap them in plastic bags, and store in the refrigerator or a cool place.

One of the best ways to keep apples is in the form of applesauce, which you can freeze: see page 88 for Beverly Cox's recipe. Or you can make apple butter and seal it in jars. This recipe makes a sweet condiment for the Pennsylvania Dutch dinner on pages 20–21.

Apple butter, like cider, is best made with a blend of different apples. Use sweet-tart, moist-soft, and dry-hard types for a well-balanced condiment. Choose at least two different varieties.

Apple Butter

5 pounds apples (two or more varieties)
1 to 2 quarts cider
Cinnamon
Allspice
Ground cloves
1 cup sugar (optional)

1. Quarter and core apples but do not peel them.
2. In large, heavy-bottomed pot, place apples and cider. Cook over low heat until apples are completely soft, stirring to prevent burning. Strain through food mill.
3. Return the puréed apples to the pot and add spices to taste. Add sugar to taste, bearing in mind that the butter will be sweeter once it has reduced and cooked more. (The natural sweetness or tartness of the mixture depends on the type of apples used. Most likely you will need little or no sugar.)
4. Cook apples until thick and smooth, stirring often to prevent burning.
5. Pack in sterilized glass jars and let cool. Seal with paraffin and store in a cool, dark place.

Today's cooks in the states of Oregon and Washington owe a debt to the pioneers who brought along their ethnic recipes, particularly to the Norwegians, Swedes, Finns, and Japanese who settled in Washington—and who learned to tame the wild grape and berry crops, converting them to pies, tarts, and turnovers. Northwestern cookery, like that of California, is also based on fresh and abundant seafood, wild game, vegetables, and fruits, as well as on delicacies from the dairy, including Tillamook, a rich, Cheddar-like cheese. In this volume, Susy Davidson and Richard Nelson have contributed West Coast menus that are notably fresh and uncomplicated.

America's forty-ninth and fiftieth states, Alaska and Hawaii, do not fit into the country's regional jigsaw, yet most Americans eat such Polynesian foods as pineapples, coconuts, and bananas. Visitors to Alaska will discover other gastronomic treats: mooseburgers, seafood delicacies, whale steaks, and enormous vegetables that thrive during the short but sun-filled growing season.

COOKING TECHNIQUES

Sautéing

Sautéing is a form of quick frying, with no cover on the pan. In French, *sauter* means "to jump," which is what vegetables or small pieces of food do when you shake the sauté pan. The purpose is to lightly brown the food and seal in the juices before further cooking. Patricia Lenz uses this technique in her recipe for Sautéed Breast of Duck with Raspberries (pages 41–42). This technique has three critical elements: the right pan, the proper temperature, and dry food.

The sauté pan: A proper sauté pan is 10 to 12 inches in diameter and has 2- to 3-inch straight sides that allow you to turn food pieces and still keep the fat from spattering. It has a heavy bottom that slides easily over a burner.

The best material (and the most expensive) for a sauté pan is tin-lined copper because it is a superior heat conductor. Stainless steel with a layer of aluminum or copper on the bottom is also very efficient. (Stainless steel alone is a poor conductor.) Heavy-gauge aluminum works well but will discolor acid food such as tomatoes. Therefore, you should not use aluminum if the food is to be cooked for more than twenty minutes after the initial browning. An-

other option is to select a heavy-duty sauté pan made of strong, heat-conductive aluminum alloys. This type of professional cookware is smooth and stick-resistant.

The ultimate test of a good sauté pan is whether or not it heats evenly; hot spots will burn the food rather than brown it. A heavy sauté pan that does not heat evenly can be saved. Rub the pan with a generous amount of vegetable oil. Then place a half inch of salt in the pan and heat it slowly over low heat, about 10 to 15 minutes, until very hot. Empty salt, do not wash the pan, and rub it with vegetable oil again.

Select a sauté pan large enough to hold the pieces of food without crowding. The heat of the fat, and air spaces around and between the pieces, facilitate browning. Crowding results in steaming—a technique that lets the juices out rather than sealing them in. If your sauté pan is not large enough to prevent crowding, separate the food into two batches, or use two pans at once.

You will find sauté pans without covers for sale, but be sure you buy one with a tight-fitting cover. Many recipes call for sautéing first, then lowering the heat and cooking the food, covered, for an additional 10 to 20 minutes. Make sure the handle is long and comfortable to hold.

When you have finished sautéing, never immerse the hot pan in cold water; this will warp the metal. Let the pan cool slightly, then add water and let it sit until you are ready to wash it. Use a wooden spatula or tongs to keep food pieces moving in the pan as you shake it over the burner. If the food sticks, as it occasionally will, a metal turner will loosen it best. Turn the pieces so that all surfaces come into contact with the hot fat and none of them sticks. Do not use a fork when sautéing meat; piercing the pieces will cause the juices to run out and will toughen the meat.

The fat: A combination of half butter and half vegetable oil or peanut oil is perfect for most sautéing; it heats to high temperatures without burning and allows you to have a rich butter flavor at the same time. Always use unsalted butter for cooking; it tastes better and will not add unwanted salt to your recipe.

Butter alone makes a wonderful-tasting sauté, but butter, whether salted or unsalted, burns at a high tempera-

11

ture. If you prefer an all-butter flavor, *clarify* the butter before you begin. This means removing the milky residue, which is the part that scorches. To clarify, heat the butter in a small saucepan over medium heat and, using a cooking spoon, skim off the foam as it rises to the top and discard it. Keep skimming until no more foam appears. Pour off the remaining oil, making sure to leave the milky residue at the bottom of the pan. The oil is clarified butter: use this for sautés.

Some sautéing recipes call for olive oil, which imparts a delicious and distinctive flavor of its own and is less sensitive than butter to high heat. Nevertheless, even the finest olive oil has some residue of fruit pulp, which will scorch at high heat. Watch carefully when you sauté in olive oil. Discard any scorched oil and start with fresh if necessary.

To sauté properly, heat the fat until it is hot but not smoking. When you see small bubbles on top of the fat, it is almost hot enough to smoke. In that case, lower the heat. When using butter and oil together, add the butter to the hot oil. After the foam from the melting butter subsides, you are ready to sauté. If the temperature is just right, the food will sizzle when you add it.

Pan Frying

Sometimes referred to as pan broiling, this technique is similar to sautéing. Food cooks in a small amount of fat, which has been preheated in a heavy skillet. Pan frying is a quick method that retains juices—it is suitable for thin-cut chops, steaks, and other foods that might dry out under a broiler. See Patricia Lenz's pan-fried hamburgers (page 45) as an example.

Poaching

You poach fish or chicken, even fruit, exactly as you would an egg—in very hot liquid in a shallow pan on top of the

---

Making Chicken Stock

Although canned chicken broth or stock is all right for emergencies, homemade chicken stock has a rich flavor that is hard to match. Moreover, the commercial broths—particularly the canned ones—are likely to be oversalted.

To make your own stock, save chicken parts as they accumulate and put them in a bag in the freezer; then have a rainy-day stock-making session, using one of the recipes here. The skin from a yellow onion will add color; the optional veal bone will add extra flavor and richness to the stock.

Basic Chicken Stock

3 pounds bony chicken parts, such as wings, back, and neck
1 veal knuckle (optional)
3 quarts cold water
1 yellow unpeeled onion, stuck with 2 cloves
2 stalks celery with leaves, cut in two
12 crushed peppercorns
2 carrots, scraped and cut into 2-inch lengths
4 sprigs parsley
1 bay leaf
1 tablespoon fresh thyme, or 1 teaspoon dried
Salt (optional)

1. Wash chicken parts and veal knuckle (if you are using it) and drain. Place in large soup kettle or stockpot (any big pot) with the remaining ingredients—except salt. Cover pot and bring to a boil over medium heat.

2. Lower heat and simmer stock, partly covered, 2 to 3 hours. Skim foam and scum from top of stock several times. Add salt to taste after stock has cooked 1 hour.

3. Strain stock through fine sieve placed over large bowl. Discard chicken pieces, vegetables, and seasonings. Let stock cool uncovered (this will speed cooling process). When completely cool, refrigerate. Fat will rise and congeal conveniently at top. You may skim it off and discard it or leave it as protective covering for stock.

Yield: About 10 cups.

The flavor of chicken stock comes from the bones (as well as the seasonings and vegetables) rather than the meat. The longer you cook the bones, the better the stock. If you would like to poach a whole chicken and want to make a good, strong stock at the same time, this highly economical recipe will accomplish both aims at once.

Strong Chicken Stock

10 cups homemade chicken stock (yield of recipe at left)
1 bay leaf
1 stalk celery
1 carrot, scraped
1 yellow onion, unpeeled
1 whole broiler or fryer (about 3 pounds)

1. Add stock, bay leaf, and vegetables to kettle large enough to hold them and chicken. Bring to a boil over medium heat.

2. Add chicken, breast up, and allow liquid to return to a simmer. Reduce heat and poach chicken with lid slightly ajar.

3. After 40 minutes, test for doneness. Insert long-handled spoon into chicken cavity and remove chicken to platter.

4. When chicken is cool enough to handle, but still warm, debone it, reserving meat for salads or sandwiches but returning skin and bones to cooking pot. Continue to simmer, uncovered, until stock has reduced by half. Proceed as in step 3 of basic stock recipe, left.

Added Touch: If you have time and want a particularly rich-looking stock, put the chicken bones in a shallow baking pan and brown them under the broiler for 10 minutes before you add them to the stock.

Stock freezes well and will keep for three months in the freezer. Use small containers for convenience and freeze in pre-measured amounts: a cup, or half a cup. Or pour the cooled stock into ice cube trays, then remove the frozen cubes and store in a plastic bag. You can drop these frozen cubes directly into your saucepan.

stove. You can use water or, better still, chicken or fish stock, or a combination of stock and white wine, or even cream, as in Susy Davidson's Salmon Stroganoff (page 51). Bring the liquid to the simmering point and add the food. Be prepared to watch carefully and to lower the heat if the liquid begins to boil. Boiling toughens meat and dries it out. Poaching is an ideal summer cooking method, since it uses so little heat.

Searing

Searing is almost the same as sautéing, but you need slightly hotter fat; when you sear, you brown the meat without shaking or stirring the pan. Heat the fat until it is very hot (at least 350 degrees), then brown the meat over high heat for a minute or two on each side. A metal turner is essential, for the meat will tend to stick. Wait until it is very brown before you turn it.

Braising

This method cooks food by moist heat, but unlike poaching or boiling, you generally brown the food well before combining it with the cooking liquid, which may be meat juice, meat stock, water, milk, or vegetable juices. Then you simmer the food and the liquid slowly over low heat in a tightly covered pot. Braising is a fine way to tenderize tough cuts of meat, and it also produces delicious vegetable dishes, such as Ann Seranne's braised celery hearts (page 81) and Susy Davidson's braised red cabbage (page 55).

Deep-Fat Frying

People often say fry when they mean sauté. But frying calls for more fat than does sautéing.

The best way to fry is to heat the fat slowly to between 360 and 375 degrees in a deep cast-iron skillet or other heavy, high-sided pan. Use a deep-fat thermometer or test the temperature by frying a small cube of bread—it should brown in less than a minute when the fat is hot enough. The temperature is important; underheating will cause the food to absorb oil, and overheating will scorch the food.

Use vegetable or peanut oil—never butter alone or a mostly butter mixture. Whatever fat you use, slide the food pieces gently into the pan, using a pair of tongs. Hot fat will spatter dangerously if you drop food into it.

Deglazing

Deglazing a pan in which food has been cooked means simply removing the food, pouring off any fat in excess of one or two tablespoons, and then, with the pan over medium heat on top of the stove, pouring liquid into it— stock, water, or wine—and reducing the liquid. As this liquid reduces, you scrape the sides and bottom of the pan with a long-handled spoon (wooden if possible) to pick up tiny bits of brown meat, congealed juices, herbs, and other good things clinging to the pan. The resulting liquid, without any thickening agent added, is basic to many of the sauces in this book; indeed, deglazing is a technique basic to most gravy and sauce making. (An additional benefit: a deglazed pan is much easier to wash.)

Broiling and Grilling

These are two relatively fast ways to cook red meat, poultry, and fish, giving the food a crisp exterior while leaving the inside juicy. For uniform cooking, flatten pieces, especially chicken or game hens, to an even thickness. Whether broiling or grilling, brush meat with melted fat, a sauce, or a marinade before you cook. This adds flavor and keeps the food moist.

In broiling, the meat cooks directly under the heat source. To ensure that the flesh is done before the skin burns, move the broiling rack five or six inches from the heat source.

In grilling, the meat cooks directly *over* the heat source, which is frequently a bed of charcoal. Set the grill far enough away from the heat so that the skin does not burn. With a good bed of coals, the right grill height might be four inches, but you must watch carefully for a few minutes to gauge the proper distance. Once the meat is browned on all sides, cover it with the grill cover (or with a tent of aluminum foil) while it cooks.

Flambéing

Flambéing makes a dramatic point at any meal. It requires igniting an already-warm, but not close to boiling, liqueur in the pan with already-cooked hot food. Be sure to remove the pan from the heat first; then avert your face and ignite the liqueur with a lighted match. A quiet flame will burn for a few seconds. Ann Seranne uses this method with her Flamed Peaches (page 81). Allow about an ounce of liqueur per person with flambéing. The taste remains, but the alcohol burns off—and you have enjoyed a moment of showmanship.

Roasting and Baking

Originally *roasting* was the term for cooking meat on a revolving spit over an open fire, but now it means cooking meat or poultry in an oven by a dry heat process. Roasting is especially suitable for thick cuts of meat and whole poultry. During the roasting process, you should baste meats several times with the drippings that collect in the pan.

Baking also means cooking food in the oven, but it is a much more versatile technique. You use it for preparing breads, for cooking a soufflé like Susy Davidson's Crab Soufflé (page 49), or for salt baking, that is, burying meat, fish, or poultry in coarse salt, as Patricia Lenz does with her Striped Bass Baked in a Salt Crust (page 39).

Steaming

A fast and low-fat way to cook vegetables and certain meats, steaming helps to preserve a food's nutrients and moisture. To steam, place vegetables—or other foods—in a steaming basket or rack over boiling liquid and cover the pan. The hot vapor, rather than the boiling water, is what cooks the food. As an example, see Beverly Cox's Steamed Broccoli Flowerets (page 88).

Pantry (for this volume)

A well-stocked, properly organized pantry is a time-saver for anyone who wants to prepare great meals in the shortest time possible. Location is the critical factor for staple storage. Whether your pantry consists of a small refrigerator and two or three shelves over the sink or a large freezer, refrigerator, and whole room just off the kitchen, you must protect staples from heat and light.

In maintaining or restocking your pantry, follow these rules:

1. Store staples by kind and date. Canned goods need a separate shelf, or a separate spot on the shelf. Put the oldest cans in front, so that you need not examine each one as you pull it out. Keep track of refrigerated and frozen staples by jotting the date on the package or writing it on a bit of masking tape.

2. Store flour, sugar, and other dry ingredients in canisters or jars with tight lids, where they will last for months. Glass and clear plastic allow you to see at a glance how much remains.

3. Keep a running grocery list near where you cook so that when a staple such as olive oil, sugar, or flour is half gone, you will be sure to stock up.

ON THE SHELF:

Anchovies
Anchovy fillets, both flat and rolled, come oil- or salt-packed, in tins. The salt-packed anchovies must be cleaned under running water, skinned, and boned. To bone, separate the fillets with your fingers and slip out the backbone.

Baking powder

Baking soda

Chicken stock
Canned stock, or broth, is adequate for most recipes and convenient to have on hand, but you may prefer to make your own (see page 12).

Dried fruits
apricots
currants
raisins

Flours and meals
All-purpose (ground for any use from cakes to bread), bleached or unbleached. Cornmeal may be yellow or white and of varying degrees of coarseness. The stone-ground variety is milled to retain the germ of the corn; it generally has a superior flavor.

Herbs and spices
Fresh herbs are always best; the flavor is much better than in dried herbs. Many fresh herbs are now available at produce markets. If you like, you can grow basil, chervil, oregano, sage, and—depending on climate—several other herbs in a small garden outdoors or on a sunny windowsill. Fresh herbs should be used immediately. The following herbs and spices, however, are perfectly acceptable in dried or packaged form—but buy in small amounts and use as quickly as possible. In measuring herbs, remember that three parts of fresh herbs will equal one part dried. *Note:* Dried chives and parsley should not be on your shelf, since they have little or no flavor. But freeze-dried chives are acceptable.

allspice
basil, fresh and dried
caraway seeds
chervil
chives, fresh, freeze-dried, or frozen
cinnamon (ground)
cloves, whole or ground
coriander
cumin
curry powder, preferably imported
dill, fresh and dried
ginger (ground)
marjoram
mustard (dry)
nutmeg, whole or freshly ground
oregano
paprika
pepper
black, whole peppercorns
These are ripe peppercorns dried in their black skins. Grind with a pepper mill for each use.

red pepper flakes
Also called crushed red pepper.

red chili peppers, dried
Cayenne pepper
ground red chili peppers
white, whole peppercorns
These are like the black variety but are dried without the dark skin. Use them in pale sauces when black pepper specks would spoil the appearance.

rosemary, fresh or dried
saffron
Made from the dried stamens of a species of crocus, this expensive seasoning adds both color and flavor.

sage
salt
Use coarse—also known as Kosher—salt because of its superior flavor and coarse texture. It is pure salt with no additives. Kosher salt and sea salt taste saltier than table salt. When the recipe calls for Kosher or sea salt, you can substitute in the following proportions: three quarters teaspoon Kosher or sea salt equals one teaspoon table salt.

savory
tarragon
thyme, leaf and ground

Honey

Hot pepper sauce

Oils
corn, peanut, or vegetable
Because these neutral oils add little or no taste to the food and have high smoking points, they are good for sautéing.

olive oil
Sample French, Greek, Spanish, and Italian oils (Luccan oil, from the Tuscan region, is sure to be in your supermarket) until you find the taste you like best. Each has its own flavor. Buy only virgin or first-pressing oil; the oil from the second pressing is full of fruit pulp that burns at high heat. Good olive oils may vary in color from green to golden yellow. The pale and less expensive oils are fine for cooking.

safflower oil
A polyunsaturated oil, especially favored by those on a low-cholesterol diet.

walnut oil
Strong, nutty flavor. Because it is expensive and does not keep well, you should buy it in small quantities. Specialty stores and some supermarkets stock it.

Onions
Store all dry-skinned onions in a cool, dry place.

garlic
The most pungent of the onion family. Garlic powder

and garlic salt are no substitute for the real thing.

leeks
Subtle onion flavor, used for soups and in sautés. Store leeks in the refrigerator.

red onions
Their sweet flavor makes them ideal for salads. For cooking, they are very mild.

scallions
Also called green onions. Mild flavor. Use the white bulbs as well as the fresh green tops. Wrap in plastic and store in the refrigerator, or chop coarsely, wrap in plastic, and freeze.

shallots
A sweet and delicate cross between onions and garlic. Use chopped for best flavor. Buy the largest shallots you can find; they are easier to peel and chop.

Spanish onions
Sweet, delicate taste. Good used in onion soups or sliced, in sandwiches.

white onions
Also called boilers or silver skins, these small round onions are suitable for cooking whole.

yellow onions
The all-purpose cooking onion; strong flavor—good for flavoring stock.

Pasta and noodles, dried or fresh
Many traditional recipes call for a special shape of pasta, as in Raymond Sokolov's recipe (page 33), which specifies fusilli—small spirals in the form of thin spaghetti. Whatever the choice, follow instructions on the package for cooking, add pasta to the pot slowly enough so that the boil is not interrupted, and avoid overcooking.

Potatoes

Rice
long-grain white rice
Lighter and fluffier than short grain when cooked.

Soy sauce
Buy the Japanese brands, which are very flavorful and less salty than Chinese and American soy sauces.

Sugar
brown sugar
confectioners' sugar
granulated sugar

Tomatoes
Italian plum tomatoes
For tomato sauces, canned plum tomatoes are an acceptable substitute for ripe tomatoes.

tomato paste
Also for sauces. With canned paste, spoon out unused portions in one-tablespoon amounts onto wax paper and freeze, then lift the frozen paste off and store in a plastic container. Sometimes available in tubes, which can be refrigerated and kept after a small amount is used.

tomato sauce

Vanilla extract

Vinegars
apple cider vinegar (also called cider vinegar)
Made from apple juice; mild in flavor.

red and white wine vinegars
Made from wines; used in cooking and salad dressings.

sherry wine vinegar
Nutty, and somewhat stronger flavored than most wine vinegars. Buy in specialty stores.

tarragon vinegar
A white or red wine vinegar flavored with fresh tarragon.

Wines, liquors
imported Marsala, or sweet sherry
red wine, sweet and dry
vermouth, dry
white wine, dry

Worcestershire sauce

IN THE REFRIGERATOR:

Bread crumbs
You need never buy these. For fresh bread crumbs, use fresh or day-old bread; for dry, use fresh to 4-day-old bread. To dry bread, toast in a 250-degree oven until golden. Process in a food processor or blender.

Butter
Unsalted is best for cooking because it does not burn as quickly as salted, and it has a sweeter flavor. Can be kept frozen until needed.

Celery

Cheese
Cheddar cheese, sharp
A firm cheese, ranging in color from nearly white to yellow. Cheddar is a versatile cooking cheese.

goat cheese, log type
Can buy either plain or with ash. Goat cheese, or *chèvre*, has a distinct, pungent taste. It comes in many shapes (for example, a log), either plain or rolled in finely powdered ash. The ash gives it a slightly salty taste.

Monterey Jack cheese
From California—a mild cheese made from skim, partly skim, or whole milk. Ideal for cooking, eating, and grating.

Parmesan cheese
Avoid the preground variety; it is very expensive and almost flavorless. Buy Parmesan by the half- or quarter-pound wedge and grate as needed: a quarter pound produces one cup of grated cheese. American Parmesans are acceptable and less costly than imported. Romano is another substitute—or try mixing the two. If you have a specialty cheese shop nearby, ask for Asiago or Kasseri cheese; they are comparable to Parmesan but less expensive.

ricotta cheese
This white, slightly sweet soft cheese, whose name means "recooked," is a by-product made from whey. It is available fresh (made from whole milk) or dry. It resembles good-quality small-curd cottage cheese, which can be substituted.

Cream
light, or half-and-half
heavy
sour cream

Eggs
Will keep up to 6 weeks. Before beating eggs, bring them to room temperature for fluffiest results.

Ginger, fresh
Buy fresh in the produce section. Slice only what you need. The rest will stay fresh in the refrigerator for 6 weeks wrapped in plastic. Or place the whole ginger root in a small jar and cover it with dry sherry to preserve it. It will keep indefinitely. You need not peel ginger root.

Lemons
In addition to its many uses in cooking, fresh lemon juice, added to cut fruits and vegetables, keeps them from turning brown. Added to the cooking water, lemon juice keeps rice from turning yellow as it cooks. Do not substitute bottled juice or lemon extract.

Mayonnaise
Although commercially prepared mayonnaise is adequate for most recipes, homemade certainly has a better flavor, and you can make it quickly and easily.

Milk

Mustards
Select the pungent Dijon variety for cooking. The flavor survives heating. Dry mustard and regular hot dog mustard have their uses and their devotees, but the recipes in this book call for Dijon.

Parsley
Put in a glass of water and cover loosely with a plastic bag. It will keep for a week in the refrigerator. Or you can wash it, dry it, and refrigerate it in a small plastic bag with a dry paper towel inside to absorb any moisture.

Yogurt, plain

Equipment

Proper cooking equipment makes the work light and is a good cook's most prized possession. You can cook expertly without a store-bought steamer or even a food processor, but basic pans, knives, and a few other items are indispensable. Below are the things you need and some attractive options for preparing the menus in this volume.

Pots and pans

Large kettle or stockpot

3 skillets (large, medium, small), with covers

Sauté pans, 10–12 inches in diameter, with covers and oven-proof handles

3 saucepans with covers (1-, 2-, and 4-quart capacities)
Choose enamel cast iron, plain cast iron, aluminum-clad stainless steel, and heavy aluminum (but you need at least one skillet that is not aluminum). Best—but very expensive—is tin-lined copper.

Broiler pan with rack

2 shallow baking pans (8″ by 8″ and 13″ by 9″ by 2″)

2 cookie sheets (11″ by 17″ and 15½″ by 12″)

Loaf pan (8½″ by 4¼″ by 3″)

2 soufflé dishes (1½-quart, 2-quart)

2- or 3-quart casserole with cover

10″ pie plate

Knives

A carbon-steel knife takes a sharp edge but tends to rust. You must wash and dry it after each use; otherwise it can blacken food and counter tops. Good-quality stainless-steel knives, frequently honed, are less trouble and will serve just as well in the home kitchen. Never put a fine knife in the dishwasher. Rinse it, dry it, and put it away—but not loose in a drawer. Knives will stay sharp and last a long time if they have their own storage rack.

Small paring knife (sharp-pointed end)

10- to 12-inch chef's knife

Boning knife

Thin-bladed slicing knife

Other cooking tools

Long-handled cooking spoon

Long-handled slotted spoon

Long-handled wooden spoon

Long-handled, 2-pronged fork

Pair of metal tongs

Wooden spatula (for stirring hot ingredients)

Metal turner (for lifting hot foods from pans)

Rubber or vinyl spatula (for folding in hot or cold ingredients, off the heat)

3 mixing bowls in graduated sizes

2 sets of measuring cups and spoons in graduated sizes (one for dry ingredients, another for shortening and liquids)

Sieve, coarse mesh

Strainers (preferably two, in fine and coarse mesh)

Colander, with a round base (stainless steel, aluminum, or enamel)

Food mill, ricer, or potato masher

Grater (metal, with several sizes of holes; a rotary grater is handy for hard cheese)

Nutmeg grater

Wooden chopping board

Vegetable peeler

Vegetable steamer

2 wire whisks

Nutcrackers

Pestle

Aluminum foil

Cheesecloth

Paper towels

Plastic wrap

Soup ladle

Waxed paper

Kitchen scissors

Kitchen timer

Toothpicks

Electric appliances

Blender or food processor

A blender will do most of the work required in this volume, but a food processor will do it more quickly and in larger volume. A food processor should be considered a necessity, not a luxury, for anyone who enjoys cooking.

Optional

Barbecue grill

Apple corer

Corn stick pan

Lobster steamer

Bread knife (serrated edge)

Carving knife

Clam or oyster knife

Light Chinese cleaver

Citrus juicer (the inexpensive glass kind from the dime store will do)

Copper bowl

Deep fryer

Deep-fat thermometer

Mandoline

Melon baller

Pastry brush for basting (a small, new paintbrush that is not nylon serves well)

Poultry pins or bamboo skewers

Roll of masking tape or white paper tape for labeling and dating

Salad spinner

Zester

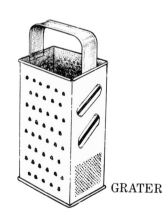

GRATER

STRAINER

SAUCEPANS

CASSEROLE

NUTMEG GRATER

SAUTÉ PAN

WHISK

PARING KNIFE

CHEF'S KNIFE

VEGETABLE STEAMER

SHARPENING STEEL

VEGETABLE PEELER

LONG-HANDLED WOODEN SPOON

SLOTTED METAL SPOON

METAL COLANDER

17

Deirdre Davis

MENU 1 (Left)
Pennsylvania Dutch Chicken
Fried Tomatoes
Saffron Noodles

MENU 2
New England Fish Chowder
Corn Sticks
Two-Cabbage Salad

MENU 3
Ham Loaf
Apple-Raisin Compote
Corn Fritters
Mixed Green Salad

Although Deirdre Davis has studied classical French cooking in both the United States and France, she admits she loves American food more, and because of her involvement with it, she has added another facet to her food career. Besides being a chef and cooking instructor, she is studying the history of American food and, in particular, that of New England. She does not view America as one vast culinary melting pot but instead thinks that regionalism and local ingredients are the most important aspects of American cooking. As one focus of her food studies, she is examining the development of Yankee cooking: how the colonists and American Indians interchanged foods and cooking methods.

She has assembled the three menus here with an eye to both the history of a recipe and how it represents its region. Menu 1 highlights Pennsylvania Dutch cooking, one of the most enduring American regional cooking styles. The Pennsylvania Dutch of Lancaster County, who are not Dutch at all but of German descent, have added many lavish yet subtly seasoned recipes to American cooking. One of the outstanding characteristics of Pennsylvania Dutch cuisine is its artful combination of sweet-sour tastes, both in the main course and in the traditional condiment tray of "seven sweets and seven sours."

Fish chowder has been popular since colonial days. The chowder of Menu 2 is a simple and mildly seasoned version. A chowder is always thickened with potatoes.

Menu 3 features several all-American favorites: ham and pork, apples, corn, and green salad.

This Pennsylvania Dutch meal of spicy chicken, fried tomatoes, and saffron noodles is accompanied by an assortment of condiments and relishes (clockwise from bottom left): baby corn, watermelon pickles, apple butter, cucumber pickles, and chowchow.

19

Pennsylvania Dutch Chicken
Fried Tomatoes
Saffron Noodles

Deirdre Davis's peppery and spicy chicken is a modification of the traditional Pennsylvania Dutch *hasenpfeffer*, which calls for rabbit. This is a plan-ahead menu because the chicken must marinate for at least one day, preferably for two, in a container in the refrigerator. Cover the container loosely with foil or plastic wrap. This long soaking tenderizes the chicken and allows it to absorb flavor. Buy a broiler, and cut it into eight pieces: two breasts, two drumsticks, two thighs, and two wings.

Other typical Pennsylvania Dutch dishes are the egg noodles seasoned with saffron—an important spice in Pennsylvania Dutch cookery—and fried tomatoes sweetened with sugar and moistened with pan drippings and heavy cream. Do not use overly ripe tomatoes.

A "seven sweets-seven sours" condiment selection is an integral part of Pennsylvania Dutch hospitality at most meals. A cook need not serve any set combination of condiments, nor need there be seven of each taste. A typical offering might include spiced watermelon rind, bread-and-butter pickles, pickled baby corn, mustardy chowchow, and apple butter, any of which you can buy in a supermarket or specialty food shop. If you have time, try Deirdre Davis's recipe for apple butter (page 10).

WHAT TO DRINK

Select a light white wine with a touch of sweetness, such as a Moselle. Or try a semi-dry California Chenin Blanc or Colombard.

SHOPPING LIST AND STAPLES

2½- to 3-pound chicken
4 large green or not-too-ripe red tomatoes
1 large onion
1 lemon
1 small bunch fresh parsley, preferably flat-leaf
½ pint heavy cream
1 stick plus 4 tablespoons unsalted butter
2 tablespoons vegetable oil
Oil or lard (for frying chicken)
½ cup apple cider vinegar
12-ounce package egg noodles, or fresh egg pasta
2½ cups flour (approximately)
1 tablespoon sugar
½ teaspoon ground ginger
¼ teaspoon ground cloves
¼ teaspoon saffron threads or 1 tablespoon Dijon mustard

Freshly grated nutmeg
Dash Cayenne pepper
Salt and freshly ground pepper

UTENSILS

Stockpot or kettle
12-inch heavy-gauge sauté pan with cover
10-inch heavy-gauge sauté pan
Large saucepan
2 heatproof platters
2 large, flat plates
9-by-12-by-3 inch baking dish
Medium-size bowl
Colander
Measuring cups and spoons
Chef's knife
Paring knife
Metal spatula
Wooden spoon
Metal tongs

START-TO-FINISH STEPS

One or two days before dinner or at least 6 to 8 hours in advance: Cut chicken into 8 serving pieces and follow chicken recipe step 1.

1. Follow chicken recipe step 2. Bring 6 tablespoons butter to room temperature for saffron noodles.
2. Follow fried tomatoes recipe step 1 and saffron noodles recipe step 1.
3. Preheat oven to 200 degrees. Follow chicken recipe steps 3 and 4.
4. While chicken is cooking, bring water to a boil for saffron noodles, step 2. Follow fried tomatoes recipe steps 2 and 3.
5. Follow saffron noodles recipe steps 3 and 4.
6. Follow chicken recipe step 5.
7. Follow fried tomatoes recipe steps 4 and 5, saffron noodles recipe step 5, chicken recipe step 6, and serve.

RECIPES

Pennsylvania Dutch Chicken

2½- to 3-pound chicken, cut into 8 serving pieces
½ cup apple cider vinegar

Dash Cayenne pepper
½ teaspoon ground ginger
¼ teaspoon ground cloves
2 tablespoons vegetable oil
1 large onion, sliced
1 lemon, sliced
Oil or lard for frying
1 to 1½ cups flour (approximately) for dredging
Salt and freshly ground pepper
Fresh parsley sprigs, preferably flat-leaf, for garnish
  (optional)

1. Arrange chicken pieces in single layer in baking dish. Pour vinegar over chicken and turn to coat the pieces. Sprinkle Cayenne, ginger, and cloves over the chicken, drizzle on 2 tablespoons oil, and cover with onion and lemon slices. Cover chicken and marinade; refrigerate. Turn the chicken pieces in the marinade often.
2. Remove chicken from refrigerator and bring to room temperature about 30 minutes before cooking.
3. When ready to cook, add oil to, or melt lard in, 12-inch heavy-gauge sauté pan to a depth of ¾ to 1 inch and heat over high heat. Pat chicken pieces dry. Put flour on flat plate. Dredge chicken pieces in the flour and shake off any excess. The chicken should be just lightly coated.
4. Cook chicken pieces in the hot fat, turning with tongs to brown evenly. When chicken is a deep crusty brown, reduce heat and cover. Move white pieces on top of the dark meat, which takes longer to cook. After about 10 minutes, check white meat for doneness with tip of knife. (The juice should run clear.) Remove breasts to heatproof platter lined with paper towels and keep warm in preheated 200-degree oven.
5. Cover sauté pan and continue to cook thighs, drumsticks, and wings over medium heat until tender and juices run clear. It will take about 30 minutes' total cooking time.
6. Drain well on paper towels and arrange the chicken pieces on a serving platter. Season with salt and pepper, and garnish with parsley sprigs, if desired.

Fried Tomatoes

4 large green or not-too-ripe red tomatoes
1 cup flour (approximately) for dredging
Salt and freshly ground pepper
1 tablespoon sugar
6 tablespoons unsalted butter
¾ cup heavy cream

2 tablespoons chopped fresh parsley, for garnish
  (optional)

1. Core tomatoes and cut into thick slices.
2. Put flour on flat plate and season with salt and pepper. Dredge tomato slices in the flour to coat each well; shake off any excess. Sprinkle sugar on both sides of the slices.
3. Heat 2 tablespoons of the butter in 10-inch heavy-gauge sauté pan and brown a few tomato slices at a time on both sides, carefully turning them with metal spatula. When done, remove the slices to a heatproof platter and keep warm in oven. Add more butter to pan as needed and continue to brown the tomato slices on both sides until all are done.
4. Add cream to pan and bring to a boil. Scrape pan with wooden spoon to loosen any brown bits on bottom. Reduce cream slightly—this will take about 10 minutes. Season with salt and pepper to taste.
5. Remove tomatoes from oven and pour sauce over them. Sprinkle with chopped parsley, if desired.

Saffron Noodles

6 tablespoons unsalted butter, at room temperature
¼ teaspoon crushed saffron threads, or 1 tablespoon
  Dijon mustard
Salt and freshly ground pepper
2 tablespoons heavy cream
2 tablespoons chopped parsley
Pinch freshly grated nutmeg
12-ounce package egg noodles, or fresh egg pasta

1. Using fork, cream butter with saffron, salt, and pepper in medium-size bowl until very light. Blend in cream, parsley, and nutmeg. Taste for seasoning and let rest to blend flavors.
2. In stockpot or kettle, bring 3 quarts of water to a boil.
3. Salt the water and add noodles, stirring to separate. Cook 7 to 10 minutes if using dried pasta, or about half that time if using fresh.
4. In large saucepan, heat 1 teaspoon of the saffron butter over medium heat.
5. Drain noodles in colander and add them to the saucepan. Add remaining butter and toss well to melt butter and coat noodles. Taste and correct seasoning, and serve immediately.

Note: if the noodles sit, the butter will tend to separate, making the noodles greasy.

New England Fish Chowder
Corn Sticks
Two-Cabbage Salad

A lettuce-lined bowl sets off the salad; parsley and snipped chives are an effective garnish for the chowder.

S ince colonial days, a traditional Friday-night supper in New England has been a steaming bowl of fish chowder. Deirdre Davis uses slab bacon in her version; if you wish, you can substitute thick-sliced bacon.

For the corn sticks, you can use a muffin tin; bake the corn muffins 30 minutes in a 350-degree oven.

WHAT TO DRINK

This home-style menu can be served with cold beer or with a simple wine, such as an Italian Verdicchio or a French Muscadet.

SHOPPING LIST AND STAPLES

½ pound slab bacon
2 to 2½ pounds white-fleshed fish fillets, such as cod, haddock, or ocean perch
2 onions
1 red onion
1 large potato (about ½ pound)
1 small head red cabbage
1 small head white cabbage
1 small bunch fresh parsley
2 eggs

1 cup milk or ½ cup light cream
1 cup buttermilk
½ pint heavy cream
1 stick plus 4 tablespoons unsalted butter
2 eight-ounce bottles clam juice
1 to 1½ cups salad oil
¼ cup cider vinegar
2 tablespoons Dijon mustard
2 cups cornmeal, or 1 cup cornmeal and 1 cup corn flour
½ teaspoon baking soda
¼ teaspoon thyme
Salt and freshly ground pepper

UTENSILS

Large, heavy-gauge saucepan
Corn stick pan
2 large bowls
1 small bowl
Measuring cups and spoons
Chef's knife
Paring knife
Slotted spoon
Wooden spoon
Soup ladle
Wire whisk

START-TO-FINISH STEPS

1. Follow corn sticks recipe steps 1 through 3.
2. Slice red onion half thinly, chop parsley, and follow cabbage salad recipe steps 1 through 3.
3. Cut slab bacon into ⅓-inch dice and follow fish chowder recipe step 1.
4. Bake corn sticks, step 4.
5. Slice onions, peel and dice potato, and follow fish chowder recipe steps 2 through 6.
6. Follow corn sticks recipe step 5, taste cabbage salad for seasoning, step 4, and serve with the hot chowder.

RECIPES

New England Fish Chowder

½ pound slab bacon, cut into ⅓-inch dice
6 tablespoons unsalted butter
2 onions, sliced
Salt and freshly ground pepper
¼ teaspoon thyme
1 large potato, peeled and cut into ½-inch dice (about 1½ cups)
2 eight-ounce bottles clam juice
1 cup heavy cream
2 to 2½ pounds white-fleshed fish fillets, such as cod, haddock, or ocean perch

1. Place bacon in large, heavy saucepan and render it over medium heat. Brown bacon in the rendered fat and remove with slotted spoon to paper towels to drain. Set aside.

Pour off all but 2 tablespoons of the fat.
2. Melt 2 tablespoons of the butter in the saucepan and add onion slices. Season with salt, pepper, and thyme, and sauté until onions are soft and lightly golden but not browned.
3. Add potatoes and toss with the onions.
4. Add fish stock or clam juice and cream, and bring to a boil. Simmer, covered, until the potatoes are just tender, about 5 to 7 minutes.
5. Wipe fish with damp paper towels and cut into 1½-inch pieces. When potatoes are tender, add fish and reserved bacon. Poach fish until tender, 5 to 10 minutes, being careful not to overcook it. Maintain heat at a simmer.
6. Correct seasoning and ladle the chowder into warmed bowls. Top each portion with generous pat of butter.

Corn Sticks

2 cups cornmeal, or 1 cup cornmeal and 1 cup corn flour
1 teaspoon salt
½ teaspoon baking soda
2 eggs, lightly beaten
1 cup buttermilk
1 cup milk or ½ cup light cream
4 to 6 tablespoons melted unsalted butter (use the smaller amount if using light cream)

1. Preheat oven to 425 degrees.
2. Grease corn stick pan and put it in oven to heat.
3. Combine cornmeal, salt, and baking soda in large bowl. Make a well in center and add eggs. Start to beat with wooden spoon, gradually gathering in the cornmeal until you have a fairly thick batter. Add buttermilk, milk or cream, and melted butter, and stir until you have a smooth batter.
4. Fill hot corn stick pan with batter and bake 20 to 25 minutes, until sticks are nicely browned and crisp on bottom.
5. Serve warm with butter.

Two-Cabbage Salad

½ small head red cabbage
½ small head white cabbage
½ red onion, sliced paper thin
¼ cup cider vinegar
Salt and freshly ground pepper
2 tablespoons Dijon mustard
1 to 1½ cups salad oil
2 tablespoons chopped parsley

1. Cut cabbage halves into quarters and core. Slice each wedge crosswise into thin slivers; combine cabbages in large bowl. You should have 4 to 5 cups shredded. Cut red onion slices crosswise and toss with the cabbage.
2. Whisk vinegar, salt, pepper, and mustard in small bowl. Slowly add oil, whisking to blend. Add parsley.
3. Pour dressing over cabbage mixture and let marinate at room temperature, tossing occasionally.
4. Correct seasonings; serve in salad bowl.

Ham Loaf
Apple-Raisin Compote
Corn Fritters / Mixed Green Salad

For the meat loaf, Deirdre Davis uses three meats—ham, veal, and pork—to create an interesting taste

Leaf-patterned dinnerware is a handsome background for the ham loaf, fruit compote, crisp corn fritters, and salad. Garnish each plate with sliced cherry tomatoes and dill.

combination. She prefers a country smoked ham or a baked ham in this recipe. You can grind the meats at home, or ask your butcher to do it.

For the apple-raisin compote, the cook suggests using tart, firm apples, such as Granny Smith or Russet. She adds apple cider vinegar, apple cider, and an apple brandy,

all of which heighten the apple taste of the compote.

You can make corn "oysters" instead of corn fritters by reducing the amount of flour in the batter by 3 tablespoons and dropping the batter by spoonfuls onto a well-buttered and preheated heavy skillet. Brown "oysters" on both sides as you would pancakes and serve them hot.

WHAT TO DRINK

The pronounced flavor of ham, particularly smoked ham, needs a medium-bodied red wine. Good choices for this menu would be a California Merlot, a medium-priced St.-Emilion, or an Italian Dolcetto.

1 pound ground smoked ham, preferably raw
¼ pound ground veal shoulder
¼ pound ground fresh pork shoulder (Boston butt)
1 head soft leaf lettuce, such as Boston, Bibb, or red leaf
¼ pound young spinach leaves
4 tart, firm apples (about 1½ pounds total weight)
3 ears fresh corn, or 2 cups frozen kernels
3 onions
1 cucumber
2 large red radishes
2 scallions
1 bunch fresh parsley
1 small bunch fresh chives
2 tablespoons fresh herbs (mint, dill, tarragon, or
    chervil), or 2 teaspoons dried
1 large clove garlic
4 eggs
½ pint heavy cream
4 tablespoons unsalted butter
2 to 3 cups oil for deep frying
½ cup salad oil
5 tablespoons apple cider vinegar
3 to 5 tablespoons apple cider
2 to 4 tablespoons flour
4 slices fresh bread
½ cup golden raisins
½ teaspoon savory
½ teaspoon thyme
¼ teaspoon allspice
¼ teaspoon ground cloves
Salt and freshly ground pepper
¼ cup applejack, Calvados, or Cognac

UTENSILS

Food processor or blender
Large stockpot or kettle
Deep-fat fryer, or heavy-gauge 12-inch skillet
Large sauté pan
Small skillet
8½-by-4¼-by-3-inch loaf pan
Salad bowl
Large mixing bowl
Medium-size mixing bowl
3 small bowls

Measuring cups and spoons
Chef's knife
Paring knife
Slotted spoon
Wooden spoon
Hand mixer
Wire whisk
Deep-fat thermometer
Vegetable peeler (optional)
Apple corer (optional)
Salad spinner (optional)

START-TO-FINISH STEPS

1. Process bread (about 4 slices) in food processor or blender to measure 1 cup crumbs, chop onion, mash garlic clove, chop parsley, and snip chives for ham loaf.
2. Prepare and bake ham loaf, steps 1 through 4.
3. Follow corn fritters recipe step 1 and apple raisin compote recipe step 1.
4. Follow fritters recipe step 2.
5. Wash salad greens, step 1.
6. Follow compote recipe steps 2 through 4.
7. While apples are cooking, follow mixed green salad recipe step 2 and fritters recipe steps 3 through 5.
8. Follow salad recipe step 3 and compote recipe step 5.
9. Remove ham loaf from oven and follow step 5. Follow corn fritters recipe steps 6 and 7, compote recipe step 6, and mixed green salad recipe step 4. Serve at once.

RECIPES

Ham Loaf

1 cup fresh bread crumbs
½ cup heavy cream
1 pound ground smoked ham, preferably raw
¼ pound ground veal shoulder
¼ pound ground fresh pork shoulder (Boston butt)
2 eggs
1 onion, finely chopped
1 large clove garlic, mashed to a purée
2 tablespoons chopped fresh parsley
2 tablespoons snipped chives
½ teaspoon savory
½ teaspoon thyme
¼ teaspoon allspice
¼ teaspoon ground cloves

Salt
Freshly ground pepper

1. Preheat oven to 350 degrees.
2. In small bowl, soak bread crumbs in cream.
3. Combine meats with remaining ingredients. Add the bread crumbs and cream, and stir to combine. In small skillet, fry a small piece of the mixture to taste for seasoning. Be careful not to oversalt, as ham is already salty.
4. Grease loaf pan and turn mixture into pan. Bake 50 minutes to 1 hour, or until juices run clear and top is crusty.
5. Let meat rest 10 minutes, then unmold onto serving platter and slice.

Apple-Raisin Compote

½ cup golden raisins
¼ cup applejack, Calvados, or Cognac
4 tart, firm apples (about 1½ pounds total weight)
4 tablespoons unsalted butter
2 onions, thinly sliced
2 tablespoons apple cider vinegar
3 to 5 tablespoons apple cider (approximately)
Salt and freshly ground pepper

1. In small bowl, soak raisins in applejack to soften and plump them.
2. Peel and core apples. Cut into quarters and thinly slice each quarter.
3. Melt butter in large sauté pan and cook onions until they are translucent and begin to soften. Add apples and cook until they begin to caramelize, about 10 to 15 minutes.
4. Drain raisins and reserve the applejack. Add raisins and vinegar to pan; stir to deglaze.
5. Continue cooking until apples and onions are well browned and tender. If compote seems too dry, add reserved applejack and cider as needed during cooking.
6. Season with salt and pepper to taste. Remove from heat and serve.

Corn Fritters

3 ears fresh corn, or 2 cups frozen kernels
2 eggs
1 teaspoon salt
½ teaspoon freshly ground pepper
2 to 4 tablespoons flour
2 tablespoons heavy cream
2 to 3 cups oil for deep frying

1. If using frozen corn, follow package instructions. If using fresh corn, husk and remove silk. In large stockpot or kettle, bring 2 quarts water to a boil.
2. Cook fresh corn in rapidly boiling water about 4 minutes. Drain. When cool enough to handle, cut kernels from cobs with edge of sharp knife. There should be about 2 cups.
3. In large bowl, beat eggs with whisk or hand mixer until very foamy and light.
4. In medium-size bowl, combine salt, pepper, flour, cream, and corn kernels, and add to eggs. The batter should not be too thin. Add more flour, if necessary, just so that batter holds together. Cover and refrigerate until ready to cook.
5. Add oil to a depth of ½ to ¾ inch in deep-fat fryer or heavy skillet. Heat to 375 degrees on deep-fat thermometer.
6. Carefully add fritter batter by tablespoonfuls to the hot fat. Cook until golden, about 2 minutes. Remove with slotted spoon and drain on paper towels.
7. Serve hot.

Mixed Green Salad

1 head soft leaf lettuce, such as Boston, Bibb, or red leaf
¼ pound young spinach leaves
1 cucumber
2 scallions
2 large red radishes
3 tablespoons apple cider vinegar
Salt and freshly ground pepper
2 tablespoons chopped fresh parsley
2 tablespoons chopped fresh herbs (mint, dill, tarragon, or chervil), or 2 teaspoons dried
½ cup salad oil

1. Wash greens well and dry thoroughly with paper towels or in salad spinner. Tear into small pieces and chill.
2. Peel cucumber and slice in half lengthwise. Remove seeds and slice crosswise on bias. Trim scallions and radishes; slice thinly.
3. In small bowl, make dressing by combining all remaining ingredients, except the oil. If using dried herbs, first soak them in the vinegar to bring out their flavor. Slowly add oil, whisking constantly.
4. Combine greens, cucumber, scallions, and radishes in salad bowl, and toss with just enough dressing to coat the greens.

Raymond Sokolov

R aymond Sokolov has often traveled from his New York home to rural American communities, seeking authentic regional foods and recipes. Because of shrinking farmlands and standardized production and mass marketing of food, many traditional dishes have vanished from the American culinary scene, but he finds that bona fide regional cooks still follow old-time recipes. During his travels, he has gathered an inventory of these regional recipes, which represent a wide range of American cooking.

Menu 1 offers two Southern city dishes—an appetizer from New Orleans and a side dish from Charleston. The fried catfish main dish represents both the rural and the metropolitan South. This dinner starts off with Oysters Rockefeller, a fiery-sweet Creole dish devised by a chef at New Orleans' Antoine's restaurant in the late 1800s. He presumably named the dish after the wealthiest man he could think of: John D. Rockefeller Sr. The original recipe is still closely guarded by Antoine's, but cooks find it a challenge, and try to match its brilliance. Okra perloo—*perloo* is a Carolinian pronunciation of *pilaf,* a rice-based dish—combines okra and bacon with rice. Menu 3 also has a regional flavor. Steamed lobster and corn on the cob are two New England specialties.

As a change of pace, Menu 2 comes from our Italo-American community; pasta has been part of our diet for many decades. This meal consists of zucchini soup, fusilli with walnut sauce, and tossed salad with vinaigrette dressing.

Oysters Rockefeller—a famous New Orleans dish—is an impressive appetizer for this Southern meal. Serve the platter of fried catfish when you pass the bowl of okra perloo—rice with sliced okra and bacon.

Oysters Rockefeller
Fried Catfish
Okra Perloo

Often eaten raw, oysters are also delicious baked, roasted, fried, grilled, fricasséed, or broiled, as in this Oysters Rockefeller recipe. To prepare Raymond Sokolov's version, use freshly shucked oysters still in their lower shells, or purchase a container of loose oysters. These you must broil in heatproof containers such as scallop shells, purchased from a specialty food shop, or muffin tins. To shuck oysters yourself, grasp the rounder half of the shell in one hand, and with the other hand, insert the tip of an oyster knife into the hinge that holds the shells together. Twist the knife to open the shells; then slide it along the inside of the upper shell, freeing the meat. Discard the upper shell and remove any bits of loose shell.

Fish stores or supermarkets sell two kinds of catfish: those commercially raised in ponds at catfish farms and those caught wild from rivers. The pond-raised fish are fed a consistent diet, so they have a predictably sweet flavor. Alternates for catfish, which is somewhat oily, are pike and yellow perch.

Okra, a native African plant brought here by slaves in the eighteenth century, is a tapered, dark-green seed pod. Okra exudes a dense liquid that thickens Creole gumbos and stews. When okra is fried, as here, the liquid dries up somewhat. For this recipe, cut the okra into ½-inch slices and sauté them for 2 to 3 minutes in the cooled bacon fat. To prevent spattering, add the rice to the okra before you add the water. If you use frozen okra, do not sauté it. Instead, add the rice, water, and okra to the cooled bacon fat, and proceed with the recipe.

WHAT TO DRINK

Oysters Rockefeller demand a fine French Chablis—a *premier cru* if at all possible—or a fine California Chardonnay. With the catfish, try a Muscadet, or a California or Italian Pinot Blanc.

SHOPPING LIST AND STAPLES

2 dozen oysters in the shell, preferably, or shucked, with shells and liquor reserved
4 catfish, filleted but not skinned (about 8 ounces each)
3 strips bacon
¼ pound okra
1 small bunch scallions
1 small bunch fresh parsley
3 cloves garlic
1½ pounds fresh spinach, or 2 ten-ounce packages frozen chopped spinach
1 tube anchovy paste
4 tablespoons unsalted butter
1 to 1½ cups white cornmeal
1 cup long-grain rice
¼ cup flour
2 cups unseasoned bread crumbs
2 cups oil for frying
Cayenne pepper
Salt and freshly ground black pepper
6 tablespoons Pernod or anise-flavored liqueur

UTENSILS

Food processor or blender
Heavy-gauge 12-inch skillet
10-inch skillet
2 medium-size saucepans
11-by-17-inch cookie sheet
Heatproof platter
Large, flat plate
Colander
Measuring cups and spoons
Chef's knife
Paring knife
Clam or oyster knife (if using oysters in their shells)
Metal spatula
Wire whisk
Tongs

START-TO-FINISH STEPS

1. If using oysters in their shells, shuck and set aside. Reserve 1 cup oyster liquor.
2. Follow okra recipe step 1.
3. Follow fried catfish recipe steps 1 through 3.
4. Roughly chop green part of 3 to 4 scallions to make ½ cup. Measure out ¼ cup densely packed fresh parsley and follow oyster recipe steps 1 through 6.
5. Slice about ¼ pound fresh okra to make 1 cup and follow okra recipe steps 2 and 3. Follow oyster recipe step 7.
6. Cook oysters, steps 8 and 9, and remove from broiler. Turn off oven. Serve as appetizers.
7. About 10 minutes before okra perloo is done, cook catfish and hold in warm oven until ready to serve with the perloo.

Oysters Rockefeller

4 tablespoons unsalted butter
¼ cup flour
2 dozen oysters in the shell, preferably, or shucked, with shells and 1 cup liquor reserved
2 tablespoons anchovy paste
Salt
Cayenne pepper
1½ pounds fresh spinach, or 2 ten-ounce packages frozen chopped spinach
½ cup roughly chopped scallions, green part only
¼ cup densely packed fresh parsley
3 cloves garlic, peeled and halved
6 tablespoons Pernod or anise-flavored liqueur
2 cups unseasoned bread crumbs

1. Melt butter in heavy saucepan. When foam subsides, whisk in flour over low to medium heat and cook roux a couple of minutes. Whisking constantly, pour in reserved oyster liquor in a slow stream. Raise heat to high and cook, whisking, until sauce thickens and is smooth.
2. Whisk in anchovy paste, salt, and Cayenne. Remove pan from heat.
3. If using fresh spinach, clean thoroughly in several changes of cold water. With just the water clinging to its leaves, cook in medium-size saucepan over low heat about 5 minutes to wilt leaves. Remove and coarsely chop. Squeeze out excess liquid. If using frozen spinach, cook according to package directions in medium-size saucepan. Squeeze out excess liquid.
4. Purée scallion greens, parsley, garlic, and spinach in blender or food processor.
5. Add the green purée to the sauce. Return pan to heat and simmer about 10 minutes, or until sauce has reduced and thickened.
6. Remove from heat and stir in Pernod.
7. Preheat broiler.
8. Put oysters back in their half shells and place on cookie sheet. Broil 4 inches from heat source 3 to 5 minutes. This partially cooks the oysters and slightly dries them.
9. Remove oysters from broiler and spoon the green sauce over them; sprinkle with bread crumbs. Put oysters back under broiler just long enough to heat the sauce through and brown the crumbs.

Fried Catfish

4 catfish, filleted but not skinned (about 8 ounces each)
Salt and freshly ground black pepper
Cayenne pepper
1 to 1½ cups white cornmeal
2 cups oil for frying

1. Wipe catfish and pat dry with paper towels.
2. Sprinkle with salt, freshly ground black pepper, and Cayenne to taste. Experience will guide you in deciding how far to go with seasoning, but if you are unsure, go lightly the first time you try this recipe. This fish tastes fine lightly seasoned.
3. Put about 1 cup cornmeal on large, flat plate. Dredge catfish in cornmeal and shake off any excess. If you prefer thick coating, dredge heavily. Set fish aside a few minutes so the coating will adhere.
4. Fill heavy-gauge 12-inch skillet to depth of ½ inch with oil and heat until oil begins to smoke. Gently add fillets and fry about 5 minutes on each side, or until golden brown.
5. Remove fillets with metal spatula and drain on paper towels. Transfer to heatproof platter and keep warm in oven until ready to serve.

Okra Perloo

3 strips bacon, diced
1 cup sliced fresh okra (about ¼ pound)
1 cup raw long-grained rice
Salt and freshly ground black pepper to taste

1. Cook bacon in 10-inch skillet and drain on paper towels. Set aside.
2. Let bacon fat cool slightly; add okra and cook over low heat, about 2 to 3 minutes.
3. Add rice and 2 cups water. Cover and cook over very low heat until rice has absorbed the water, about 20 minutes.
4. Season with salt and freshly ground pepper. Turn into serving dish and garnish with bacon.

ADDED TOUCH

The editors suggest these typically Southern accompaniments for fried catfish: pickled watermelon rind, corn relish, and hush puppies. You can buy good brands of watermelon pickles and corn relish if you prefer not to make them, but hush puppies have to be homemade just before serving. Mix the batter and set out the oil before you begin preparing the rest of the meal. Then cook the hush puppies just before you broil the oysters. Cover with a kitchen towel to keep them warm until serving time.

Hush Puppies

1 cup sifted all-purpose flour
1 cup yellow cornmeal
4 teaspoons baking powder
½ teaspoon salt
1 egg, lightly beaten
⅔ cup buttermilk
⅓ cup finely chopped onion
2 to 3 cups cooking oil

1. In large mixing bowl, combine dry ingredients.
2. Lightly beat egg and add, with buttermilk and onion, to flour mixture. Combine well.
3. Heat cooking oil in Dutch oven until smoking, or until oil reaches 375 degrees on deep-fat thermometer.
4. Add batter to hot oil by rounded teaspoonfuls. Cook, turning frequently, about 3 to 5 minutes, until golden brown.

Zucchini Soup
Fusilli with Walnut Sauce
Tossed Salad Vinaigrette

Zucchini soup and fusilli with walnut sauce are accompanied by a salad garnished with beets and olives.

The main dish for this light, informal meal uses fusilli, also called rotelle, which is a corkscrew-shaped pasta. Its walnut sauce is similar to pesto. It differs from the traditional Italian pesto—a paste of basil, garlic, olive oil, pine nuts, and Parmesan cheese, used as a summer seasoning when fresh basil is on hand—because it calls for pantry staples available all year. Instead of basil and pine nuts, Raymond Sokolov blends parsley and shelled walnuts together, and adds ricotta as a thickener. Ricotta, a white, soft cheese, is like small-curd cottage cheese, which you can use as a substitute.

WHAT TO DRINK

Buy a dry California Sauvignon Blanc or a French white, such as a Sancerre, and serve lightly chilled.

SHOPPING LIST AND STAPLES

3 zucchini (about 1 pound)
1 head red-leaf lettuce
1 medium-size onion
1 bunch fresh parsley

5 tablespoons unsalted butter
8-ounce container sour cream
½ pint ricotta cheese
¼ pound Parmesan cheese
3 to 3½ cups chicken stock, preferably homemade (see page 12), or canned
10-ounce package frozen lima beans
10-ounce package frozen peas
2 tablespoons vegetable oil
1 cup plus 2 tablespoons olive oil
2 tablespoons red wine vinegar
1 pound fusilli or other pasta
1 cup shelled walnuts
Salt and pepper

UTENSILS

Food processor or blender
Stockpot or kettle
10-inch sauté pan or skillet
Large saucepan
2 small bowls
Colander
Strainer
Measuring cups and spoons
Chef's knife
Rubber spatula
Wire whisk
Cheese grater (if not using processor or blender)
Salad spinner (optional)

START-TO-FINISH STEPS

1. Follow fusilli recipe step 1, shell walnuts if necessary, and grate enough Parmesan to measure 2 tablespoons.
2. Chop onion for soup and follow steps 1 through 4.
3. If using food processor, wipe out with paper towels. Make walnut sauce for fusilli, step 2. Using rubber spatula, transfer walnut sauce to small bowl. Follow tossed salad recipe steps 1 and 2.
4. Wipe out food processor with paper towels. Follow soup recipe steps 5 through 8 and fusilli recipe step 3.
5. Follow salad recipe step 3, zucchini soup recipe steps 9 and 10, and fusilli recipe step 4. Serve immediately.

RECIPES

Zucchini Soup

3 zucchini (about 1 pound)
Salt
2 tablespoons unsalted butter
1 medium-size onion, chopped
3 to 3½ cups chicken stock
Pepper
1 cup frozen lima beans
1 cup frozen peas
1 tablespoon sour cream plus ½ cup sour cream for garnish (optional)

1. Wash and coarsely chop zucchini. In food processor or blender, purée half the chopped zucchini with pinch of salt.
2. Heat butter in sauté pan. Sauté remaining chopped zucchini and onion until softened.
3. Drain puréed zucchini in strainer set over small bowl and reserve liquid. Add the pulp to the sautéed zucchini and onion.
4. In large saucepan, bring 3 cups chicken stock to a boil.
5. Add salt and pepper to taste, lima beans, and peas. Simmer until softened, about 3 to 4 minutes.
6. Add zucchini mixture and simmer 5 minutes.
7. Remove soup from heat and let cool a few minutes. Purée in food processor or blender. Check consistency; you may need a bit more stock. Correct seasonings.
8. Add 1 tablespoon sour cream to reserved zucchini liquid and whisk it into the soup.
9. Reheat if necessary before serving, but do not boil.
10. Garnish each serving with generous dollop of sour cream, if desired.

Fusilli with Walnut Sauce

Salt
2 tablespoons vegetable oil
1 cup shelled walnuts
¾ cup fresh parsley
¾ cup olive oil
2 tablespoons grated Parmesan cheese
3 tablespoons unsalted butter, melted
3 tablespoons ricotta cheese
Pepper
1 pound fusilli or other pasta

1. In large stockpot or kettle, bring 4 quarts of lightly salted water and the vegetable oil to a boil.
2. Put walnuts, parsley, olive oil, Parmesan cheese, butter, ricotta, and salt and pepper to taste in food processor or blender. Process until smooth.
3. Add pasta to the boiling water and cook until *al dente*. Fresh pasta cooks in about 7 minutes, dried in about 10 minutes. Drain in colander and transfer to serving bowl.
4. Top with the walnut sauce; just before serving, toss to combine.

Tossed Salad Vinaigrette

1 head red-leaf lettuce
Salt and pepper
2 tablespoons red wine vinegar
6 tablespoons olive oil

1. Wash lettuce thoroughly and dry in salad spinner or pat dry with paper towels. Tear into bite-size pieces. You should have about 4 cups.
2. Put salt, pepper, and vinegar in salad bowl. Combine briskly with wire whisk. Gradually add oil, whisking to incorporate.
3. Just before serving, add the lettuce to the salad bowl and toss well.

Cheddar Cheese Soup
Steamed Lobster
Corn on the Cob

Pass ramekins of melted butter when you serve the lobster, and for extra zest, serve lemon slices on each dinner plate.

The large North American lobster, the king of shellfish, prized for its rich meat, turns any meal into a feast. Although lobsters can grow to enormous sizes, up to 45 pounds and 6 feet long, they are generally marketed when they reach 1 to 2 pounds, an ample size for one serving. You must buy lobsters live: make sure that they are very active, a sure sign of freshness, and that they are approximately the same weight, for uniform cooking. You will need a lobster steamer or large stockpot to accommodate the lobsters. Once the water boils, place the lobsters in the pot—the heat kills them instantly. Cover the pot and let the lobsters steam for 10 to 12 minutes for 1-pound lobsters, and 12 to 15 minutes for 1¼-pound lobsters. Remove the lobsters from the pot and lay them on their backs. When they are cool enough to handle, split each shell with a sharp knife from head to tail, right down the middle. Clean away the stomach and the black vein that runs lengthwise. The lobsters are now ready to serve. Be sure to provide your guests with plenty of extra napkins, a nutcracker for cracking the claws, and bowls for the empty shells.

Instead of plain melted butter, you may want to serve lemon-flavored butter with the lobsters. Cream 1 stick of unsalted butter with 1 tablespoon finely minced fresh or frozen chives, 1 teaspoon grated lemon rind, 2 tablespoons fresh lemon juice, and salt and pepper to taste.

WHAT TO DRINK

This American summer feast will taste best with cold beer or a good California Chardonnay or French white Burgundy.

SHOPPING LIST AND STAPLES

4 live lobsters (1 to 1¼ pounds each)
8 ears extremely fresh corn
1 medium-size onion
1 small bunch scallions

Fresh or frozen chives (optional)
4 sticks plus 3 tablespoons unsalted butter
1⅓ cups milk
½ pint heavy cream
½ pound sharp Cheddar cheese
2 cups chicken stock, preferably homemade (see page 12), or canned
3 tablespoons flour
1 teaspoon pickling spice, or 1 bay leaf and ½ teaspoon thyme
Salt and pepper

UTENSILS

Large steamer or 8-quart kettle with cover (for lobster)
Large stockpot or kettle with cover (for corn)
Large, heavy-gauge saucepan with cover
Small saucepan
Metal colander (if using kettle for lobster)
Coarse sieve
Measuring cups and spoons
Chef's knife
Paring knife
Wooden spoon
Cheese grater
Tongs
Kitchen scissors
4 nutcrackers

START-TO-FINISH STEPS

1. Set water to boil for corn, step 1.
2. For cheese soup, trim and chop scallions and onion, and grate Cheddar. Follow soup recipe steps 1 and 2.
3. Follow lobster recipe step 1.
4. Follow soup recipe step 3 and serve.
5. Follow lobster recipe step 2 and corn recipe step 2. Melt butter for lobsters in small saucepan over low heat.
6. Follow corn recipe step 3, and lobster recipe steps 3 and 4.
7. Follow corn recipe step 4. While guests are eating, begin second batch of corn, step 5.

RECIPES

Cheddar Cheese Soup

3 tablespoons unsalted butter
2 to 3 scallions, trimmed and chopped
½ medium-size onion, peeled and chopped
1 teaspoon pickling spice, or 1 bay leaf and ½ teaspoon thyme
3 tablespoons flour
2 cups chicken stock
½ pound sharp Cheddar cheese, grated
1⅓ cups milk
⅔ cup heavy cream
1 tablespoon chopped fresh or frozen chives for garnish (optional)

1. In large, heavy saucepan, heat butter over medium heat until foam subsides. Add scallions, onion, and pickling spice. Sauté until onion is soft. Add flour and cook, stirring, 2 minutes, or until flour no longer has a raw taste.
2. Immediately add chicken stock, cheese, milk, and cream, stirring well to combine. Slowly bring to a boil, stirring to melt cheese. Immediately reduce heat and simmer, covered, 15 minutes.
3. Remove from heat. Using wooden spoon, push the soup through coarse sieve. Serve garnished with chopped chives, if desired.

Steamed Lobster

4 live lobsters (1 to 1¼ pounds each)
Salt
2 sticks unsalted butter, melted

1. Put lobsters in steamer or 8-quart kettle to make sure that they will fit; then remove them. Fill pot to depth of 3 inches with cold water, preferably seawater. If using tap water, salt lightly.
2. Bring water to a full rolling boil. Add lobsters to steamer basket or to colander set over boiling water and cover pot. Steam 1-pound lobsters 10 to 12 minutes, 1¼-pounders 12 to 15 minutes. To be sure they are done, you can remove a lobster from the pot and crack a claw, if you wish.
3. With kitchen scissors, cut underside of tail along its middle, from stem to stern, giving guests easy access to the lobster meat. This preliminary step also facilitates draining the lobsters of residual cooking liquid before you bring them to the table.
4. Serve with individual ramekins of melted butter and nutcrackers.

Corn on the Cob

8 ears extremely fresh corn
Salt
Butter

1. In large stockpot or kettle, bring 4 quarts of salted water to a boil.
2. Husk corn, whisk away silk, break or cut off long stalks, and plunge 4 ears into the boiling salted water.
3. Cook 4 to 5 minutes after water returns to a boil, then remove with tongs.
4. Heap on serving plate and serve with salt and butter. Set a couple of sticks of butter on the table so that guests can simply roll their corn lengthwise in the butter. Speed counts.
5. To cook the remaining 4 ears, simply set them in the hot water and cover. They will be ready to serve in about 7 minutes.

Note: perfect corn in August is perfect only immediately after picking. The sweetness fades fast, so try to buy corn that has been picked the day you will use it.

Patricia Lenz

Several years ago, when many American home cooks were preoccupied with French *haute cuisine*, Patricia Lenz was concentrating on American recipes. When she opened a restaurant on Long Island, she featured all-American meals and often scoured the whole country for ingredients. Today, she is no longer a restaurant owner but still lives on Long Island, where she grows grapes and makes wine. Whenever she cooks for company, she buys seasonal Long Island ingredients, purchased from local farmstands and markets, and uses them to interpret national, American regional, and international recipes.

Each of her menus highlights the produce, poultry, or seafood for which Long Island is famous. For instance, striped bass, a popular game fish plentiful in Long Island waters, is the main course for Menu 1. Menu 2 features new potatoes and duckling—both important Long Island products. Potato farms patchwork the eastern end of Long Island. Local duck farmers produce nearly 5 million birds annually. Menu 3 starts with cherrystone clams on the half shell. The local Indians once described Long Island as "the island of shells" because of its abundant shellfish. Hard-shell clams, as cherrystones and quahogs are commonly known, account for much of this shellfish harvest.

After baking the bass in a salt crust, serve it in the bottom crust, on a platter edged with feathery stalks of dill. Put the cheese-topped rounds in a separate basket. Sautéed cherry tomatoes provide a striking color contrast.

Caesar Salad with Baked Goat Cheese
Striped Bass Baked in a Salt Crust
Cucumber Noodles / Sautéed Cherry Tomatoes

Cooking foods packed in a layer of salt is an old technique that the Chinese probably invented. The advantage of this method is that the thick salt crust traps moisture and flavor, and cuts cooking time. Surprisingly, the crust adds no salty flavor because the heat seals the exterior of the food. Do not scale the fish for this recipe.

One way to salt-pack fish is to encase it in a salt-water paste; another, as in Patricia Lenz's recipe for whole striped bass, is to bury the fish in a pile of loose salt. Since table salt is too fine to pack well, you must use Kosher salt or sea salt. For this recipe, lay the whole tarragon-flavored bass (or red snapper, if bass is not available) on a bed of salt, all on an aluminum foil-covered cookie sheet. Then pack the fish with a layer of salt before baking. After baking, carefully remove the salt crust, and brush off any loose salt. When selecting a fish, choose one with shiny, fresh-looking skin.

Caesar salad traditionally calls for Romaine lettuce, croutons, garlic, Parmesan cheese, a raw egg, anchovy fillets, and lemon juice. This version is accompanied by rounds of bread topped with baked goat cheese. Patricia Lenz recommends buying an American goat cheese; if you are unable to find one, she suggests that you use a log-shaped Montrachet.

WHAT TO DRINK

This meal needs a crisp, fruity white wine. Choose a Reisling, either a dry one from California, Washington, or Alsace, or a slightly off-dry Kabinett from Germany.

SHOPPING LIST AND STAPLES

1 whole striped bass or red snapper (about 3 pounds), unscaled, cleaned, and gutted, but with head and tail left on
1 large head Romaine
1 pint ripe cherry tomatoes
2 long seedless cucumbers, preferably, or 4 small cucumbers
3 lemons
1 clove garlic
1 large shallot
1 bunch fresh tarragon or dill
1 egg
½ pint heavy cream
4 tablespoons unsalted butter

¼ pound Parmesan cheese
4-ounce cylindrical goat cheese (American, if available)
3-ounce tin flat anchovy fillets
½ cup olive oil
2 tablespoons tarragon vinegar
Small loaf home-style white bread
¼ teaspoon sugar
12 cups Kosher salt
Freshly ground white pepper
Salt and black pepper

UTENSILS

Food processor
12-inch sauté pan
10-inch sauté pan
15½-by-12-inch cookie sheet or broiling pan
8-by-8-inch shallow baking pan
Salad bowl
Large glass or stainless steel mixing bowl
Small bowl
Colander
Measuring cups and spoons
Chef's knife
Paring knife
Mandoline (optional)
Metal spatula
Wooden spoon
Vegetable peeler
Kitchen scissors
Salad spinner (optional)

START-TO-FINISH STEPS

1. Follow cucumber recipe steps 1 and 2, and Caesar salad recipe steps 1 and 2.
2. Prepare salt-baked fish recipe, steps 1 through 3.
3. Make dressing for Caesar salad, steps 3 and 4.
4. Put fish in oven to cook, step 4.
5. Complete Caesar salad recipe, steps 5 through 8, and serve while fish is cooking.
6. Five minutes before fish is ready, follow cucumber noodles recipe steps 3 through 5.
7. Remove fish from oven, and follow step 5.
8. Cook sautéed tomatoes, steps 1 through 3, complete step 6 of cucumber noodles recipe, and serve with fish, step 6.

Caesar Salad with Baked Goat Cheese

1 large head Romaine
1 ounce Parmesan cheese
1 clove garlic, peeled
1 egg yolk
2 tablespoons fresh lemon juice
Freshly ground pepper
½ cup olive oil
4 slices home-style white bread, cut into 2½-inch rounds
4 slices goat cheese
8 anchovy fillets, rinsed and patted dry
Salt

1. Preheat oven to 450 degrees.
2. Wash lettuce and dry in salad spinner or pat dry with paper towels, and break large leaves into bite-size pieces. Leave small, pale inner leaves whole. Arrange in salad bowl and refrigerate.
3. Grate Parmesan cheese in food processor fitted with metal blade. Remove to small bowl and reserve.
4. Add garlic clove—there is no need to wash the processor between operations—and chop. Add egg yolk to the garlic and process 3 to 4 seconds. Add lemon juice and pepper to taste, and process 5 seconds. With machine running, slowly drizzle in the olive oil down the feed tube.
5. Place four bread rounds in shallow baking pan and bake in middle of oven 3 to 4 minutes, until bread is lightly golden on one side.
6. Remove pan from oven, turn bread, and toast other side. Top each piece with a slice of goat cheese. Return pan to oven and bake 5 to 8 minutes, until cheese is hot. Remove from oven, but do not turn off heat.
7. To serve, remove salad from refrigerator and toss with the dressing, anchovies, Parmesan cheese, and salt to taste, making sure to coat each leaf with dressing.
8. Serve the goat cheese-topped rounds on the side, with the salad.

Striped Bass Baked in a Salt Crust

1 whole striped bass or red snapper (about 3 pounds), unscaled, cleaned, and gutted, but with head and tail left on
12 cups Kosher salt
Fresh tarragon or dill sprigs, plus dill sprigs for garnish (optional)
2 lemons, cut in half
Salt and pepper

1. Preheat oven to 450 degrees.
2. Line cookie sheet with aluminum foil. Put half the salt on the foil so that it forms a ½-inch layer, approximately as long and as wide as the fish.
3. Place sprigs of tarragon or dill inside fish and place it on top of salt bed. Cover fish with remaining salt and pack salt down and around sides of fish. Crimp edges of foil to

keep salt from spreading, but do not cover top of fish with foil.
4. Bake 30 to 35 minutes.
5. Lift fish, still in its foil container, to large serving platter. Using scissors, trim away foil to display salt-coated fish. Then carefully and thoroughly remove the top layer of salt from the fish. Garnish with dill sprigs, if desired.
6. At the table, using 2 tablespoons, lift the skin from fish; discard skin. Remove fillet and divide into 2 servings. Next, carefully remove bones and discard. Separate remaining fillet from bottom skin and divide into 2 servings. Garnish each serving with half a lemon and pass salt and pepper.

Cucumber Noodles

2 long seedless cucumbers, preferably, or 4 small cucumbers
½ teaspoon salt
¼ teaspoon sugar
2 tablespoons tarragon vinegar
2 tablespoons unsalted butter
1 teaspoon finely minced shallot
1 teaspoon minced fresh tarragon or dill
¼ cup heavy cream
Salt and freshly ground white pepper

1. Peel cucumbers. Slice them in half lengthwise and seed, if necessary. If using long cucumbers, cut them in half crosswise. With mandoline, cut cucumbers into medium-sized noodles, about 5 inches long. If you do not own a mandoline, julienne cucumbers with chef's knife. For an easier but less glamorous presentation, cut cucumbers crosswise into ¼-inch slices.
2. Place cucumber noodles in large glass or stainless steel bowl with salt, sugar, and tarragon vinegar. Toss to coat and let macerate 20 to 30 minutes.
3. Just before serving, drain cucumbers in colander.
4. Melt butter in 12-inch sauté pan over medium heat. Add shallots and sauté 1 minute. Add drained cucumber noodles to pan. Lower heat, and cook gently 3 to 4 minutes, stirring from time to time with wooden spoon.
5. Add tarragon and heavy cream. Cook 2 to 3 minutes, stirring.
6. Add salt and pepper to taste, and serve hot.

Sautéed Cherry Tomatoes

1 pint ripe cherry tomatoes
2 tablespoons unsalted butter
Salt and freshly ground pepper

1. Rinse tomatoes and pat dry.
2. Melt butter in 10-inch sauté pan over medium heat. Add tomatoes and sauté just until warm, 1 to 2 minutes. Do not allow them to overcook, or they will become mushy and lose their shape.
3. Sprinkle with salt and pepper to taste, and serve immediately.

New Potatoes with American Caviar
Sautéed Breast of Duck with Raspberries
Steamed Broccoli

When you serve this elegant company meal, arrange the sliced duck breast with some raspberries, and pass the creamy sauce separately. A lemon slice topped with parsley and a few raspberries is an easy garnish.

Patricia Lenz's breast of duck served with a raspberry-bourbon sauce is a dramatic entrée for a company dinner. Most supermarkets sell frozen whole ducks, but because ducks are increasingly in demand, you often can find fresh duck, or even packaged fresh duck breast, the meaty part of the bird. This recipe calls for ripe raspberries as an accompaniment, but for a change of pace, Patricia Lenz suggests using instead tart, fresh cranberries, which you cook according to the raspberry recipe.

Like its thicker cousin, sour cream, crème fraîche, which tops the scooped-out new potatoes, is a cultivated cream product with a silky texture. It is costly and not readily available, even at well-stocked dairy departments, so you can either substitute sour cream or make your own crème fraîche the day before you need it. Whisk ½ pint heavy cream into ½ pint sour cream at room temperature. Pour this mixture into a glass jar, cover it tightly, let it stand in a warm place for 6 to 8 hours, and then refrigerate. It will keep for 10 days.

WHAT TO DRINK

Duck can take either a red or a white wine. Here, it would be best accompanied by a full-bodied, dry white wine, such as a California Chardonnay or French Burgundy.

SHOPPING LIST AND STAPLES

2 fresh ducks (about 5 pounds each), preferably Long Island, or frozen
1 large head broccoli
12 small new potatoes
1 lemon
1 pint fresh raspberries
Fresh chervil or thyme sprigs (optional)
Fresh dill sprigs or chives (optional)
½ pint heavy cream or crème fraîche
½ pint sour cream or crème fraîche
2 tablespoons unsalted butter
4 ounces American Atlantic sturgeon caviar, or more, depending on your budget
2 tablespoons olive oil
1 tablespoon sugar
White pepper
Dash Cayenne pepper
Salt and pepper
½ cup bourbon

UTENSILS

12-inch heavy-gauge sauté pan with cover
Large saucepan
Vegetable steamer
Heatproof platter
Heatproof medium-size bowl
Measuring cups and spoons
Chef's knife
Boning knife
Paring knife
Spatula
Wooden spoon
Vegetable scrub brush
Melon baller

START-TO-FINISH STEPS

In the morning: If using frozen ducks for entrée, remove from freezer to thaw.

1. Follow sautéed duck recipe steps 1 through 3.
2. Follow new potatoes recipe steps 1 through 3.
3. While potatoes are steaming, continue with duck recipe, steps 4 and 5.
4. Clean and prepare broccoli, step 1. Follow new potato recipe steps 4 and 5.
5. Follow broccoli recipe step 2. Juice lemon.
6. Follow sautéed duck recipe steps 6 through 10.
7. Follow steamed broccoli recipe step 3, sautéed duck recipe step 11, and serve with the new potatoes.

RECIPES

New Potatoes with American Caviar

12 small new potatoes
¼ cup sour cream or crème fraîche
4 ounces American Atlantic sturgeon caviar, or more, depending on your budget
Fresh dill sprigs or chives for garnish (optional)

1. Scrub potatoes with vegetable brush. With paring knife, remove small slice from bottom of each so that potato will stand upright. Use melon baller to hollow out section from top of each potato.
2. Set up vegetable steamer in large saucepan, add about 1 inch of water, and bring to a boil.
3. Steam potatoes 10 to 12 minutes, until they can be pierced easily with tip of knife.
4. Remove potatoes from steamer and set aside on cutting board until cool enough to handle. They are best when served lukewarm.
5. Using small measuring spoon, fill top of each potato with sour cream or crème fraîche, top with caviar, and garnish with sprigs of dill or finely minced chives, if desired.

Sautéed Breast of Duck with Raspberries

2 fresh ducks (about 5 pounds each), preferably Long Island, or frozen
2 tablespoons olive oil
Salt and white pepper
1 tablespoon sugar
2 cups fresh raspberries
½ cup bourbon
½ cup heavy cream or crème fraîche
Dash Cayenne pepper

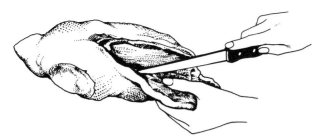

With boning knife, separate duck breast from carcass.

Trim away excess fat.

2 tablespoons unsalted butter
1 tablespoon minced fresh chervil or thyme (optional)

1. Using sharp boning knife, remove wings from ducks as close to bone as possible in order to leave maximum amount of meat on breast. Remove drumsticks.
2. To separate the breast from the carcass, locate breast-bone and make an incision the length of the ridge. Holding knife against breastbone and away from flesh, cut gently downward to remove each breast section in one piece. Place each section skin side down and trim away excess fat and skin, so that you have 4 half-heart-shaped pieces.
3. Lightly score skin and pat dry with paper towels.
4. Preheat oven to 200 degrees.
5. Heat olive oil in large, heavy sauté pan. Add duck breasts, skin side down. Cook over medium-high heat 7 to 8 minutes, or until medium rare. Do not turn breasts during cooking. Cooking them skin side down the entire time will render the maximum amount of fat from the skin and keep the flesh from becoming dry.
6. Remove breasts to heatproof platter. Sprinkle with salt and white pepper to taste and keep warm in oven.
7. Pour off all but 1 tablespoon fat from pan. Add sugar and cook over medium heat, stirring and scraping with wooden spoon, until sugar is lightly caramelized, about 2 to 3 minutes. Add raspberries and cook just until coated and warmed through. Remove from pan to heatproof bowl and keep warm in oven.
8. Add bourbon to pan. Over low to medium heat, deglaze pan by scraping with wooden spoon. Be careful that the warm bourbon does not ignite and flame. If this should happen, however, immediately cover with lid to extinguish flames. Reduce bourbon by half.
9. Add heavy cream or crème fraîche and pinch Cayenne, and simmer 2 to 3 minutes. Correct seasonings with salt and white pepper. Add half the raspberries, remove from heat, and swirl in butter.
10. Pour into sauce boat and set on table.
11. To serve, slice each duck breast with chef's knife across grain into 5 or 6 medallions. Arrange duck pieces on individual dinner plates. Garnish with remaining raspberries and minced fresh chervil or thyme, if desired, and pass the creamy raspberry sauce on the side.

Steamed Broccoli

1 large head broccoli
Juice of ½ lemon
Salt and pepper

1. Wash broccoli and divide into 4 sections. Peel stems and trim off any woody parts.
2. Bring water to a boil in vegetable steamer and steam broccoli until the stems can be pierced easily with tip of knife, about 5 to 8 minutes.
3. Remove from steamer. Sprinkle lightly with lemon juice and salt and pepper to taste.

LEFTOVER SUGGESTION

The duck thighs and legs may be reserved or frozen for use in a cassoulet or stew; the wings, neck, gizzard, and carcass may be reserved for use in stock. A rich stock is handy, since game birds produce little natural gravy. Reserve duck liver for paté.

ADDED TOUCH

Corn pancakes complement the duck and are easy to make. You can stack them between pieces of wax paper after cooking and keep them warm in a 200-degree oven. They will keep well for at least half an hour.

Corn Pancakes

2 cups frozen corn kernels (do not defrost)
¼ cup heavy cream
2 eggs
¼ cup flour
½ teaspoon baking powder
½ teaspoon sugar
¼ teaspoon white pepper
Pinch nutmeg
Pinch Cayenne
2 tablespoons unsalted butter (approximately)

1. Place all ingredients except the butter in bowl of food processor fitted with metal blade. Process 10 seconds, or until no lumps of flour remain. Remove to a pitcher and refrigerate until ready to use.
2. Heat heavy skillet or griddle over medium heat. Add 1 tablespoon of the butter and swirl to coat bottom of pan. Pour or ladle enough batter into pan to form 2-inch rounds. (A 9-inch pan should cook 6 pancakes at one time.) When edges begin to brown, turn and cook briefly on other side. Repeat process, adding butter as needed, until batter is used up.
3. As pancakes finish cooking, stack them with wax paper to separate them. Place in warm oven until ready to serve.

Clams on the Half Shell
Hamburgers Stuffed with Monterey Jack
Three-Bean Salad with Avocado

Offer clams on the half shell as an appetizer, and while your guests enjoy them, cook the hamburgers and arrange the salad on the dinner plates. Garnish the hamburgers, if you wish, with sprouts and spinach leaves.

Cherrystone clams, or quahogs, served on the half shell, are a classic American dish. Native to New England and Long Island coastal waters, these hard-shell clams taste best well chilled. After you bring the fresh clams home, scrub them with a stiff brush under cold water and discard any with cracked or broken shells. Refrigerate the clams before opening; this relaxes them and makes them easier to pry apart. Open them just before serving, using this technique: hold one in the palm of one hand, with its hinged end firmly grasped. Insert a clam knife, or any thin-bladed knife, between the upper and lower shells and cut around the edge, being sure to cut entirely through the muscle that holds the shells together. To serve, leave the clam in the bottom half of the shell and remove any bits of broken shell. To highlight their delicate flavor, season clams lightly with lemon juice and freshly ground pepper.

Hamburgers have been a nationally popular food since Americans began to eat them in the twentieth century. Hamburgers cook quickly, are ideal for picnics or informal meals, and are easy to eat. Patricia Lenz's version starts with freshly ground top-quality beef, which she stuffs with grated Monterey Jack cheese to produce a melted cheese interior. You can grill these patties outdoors, or pan fry them in olive oil.

WHAT TO DRINK

This menu sets out warm, familiar flavors very simply and directly. Serve a young, fruity California Zinfandel, a Beaujolais, or a good Chianti Classico—not a Riserva.

SHOPPING LIST AND STAPLES

1½ pounds freshly ground round steak
24 cherrystone clams
1 ripe avocado
1 medium tomato
Fresh lettuce leaves (optional)
Fresh spinach leaves (optional)
1 small red onion
2 lemons
1 lime
1 small bunch fresh parsley
Fresh oregano, basil, or coriander sprigs, or ½ teaspoon dried oregano
1 clove garlic
2 tablespoons unsalted butter (if pan frying hamburgers)
6 ounces Monterey Jack cheese
10-ounce can white kidney beans (also called cannellini)
8-ounce can red kidney beans
10-ounce can garbanzo beans (also called chick-peas)
16-ounce can golden hominy
½ cup olive oil, plus 4 tablespoons (if pan frying hamburgers)
2 tablespoons red wine vinegar
Sourdough or French bread
Salt and freshly ground black pepper
½ cup full-bodied red wine (if pan frying hamburgers)

UTENSILS

Barbecue grill or heavy-gauge 12-inch skillet with cover
Heatproof platter
Salad bowl
Large bowl
Small bowl
Metal colander
Fine-meshed strainer
Measuring cups and spoons
Paring knife
Bread knife (optional)
Clam knife (optional)
Metal spatula
Cheese grater
Scissors (optional)
4 small squares cheesecloth and white thread (optional)

START-TO-FINISH STEPS

1. If grilling hamburgers, prepare barbecue grill, hamburgers recipe step 1, and preheat oven to 200 degrees.
2. Chop fresh herbs for three-bean salad and follow steps 1 through 5.
3. For hamburgers recipe, follow either grilling steps 2 through 6 or pan frying steps 1 through 3.
4. Prepare clam recipe, steps 1 through 3, and serve.
5. For hamburgers recipe, follow either grilling steps 7 and 8 or pan frying steps 4 through 6.
6. Follow three-bean salad recipe step 6 and serve with the hamburgers.

RECIPES

Clams on the Half Shell

24 cherrystone clams
2 lemons
Lettuce leaves for garnish (optional)
Freshly ground black pepper

1. Have your fishmonger open the clams. Or, if you are so inclined, open them yourself with a clam knife, as shown in the diagrams below. Check them for stray bits of shell, but do not rinse in water, which would destroy their briny

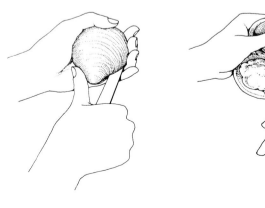

flavor. Keep chilled in large bowl until serving time. Chill 4 serving plates as well.

2. Cut each lemon in half. If desired, wrap each half in a small square of clean cheesecloth and tie ends with white thread. Cut off excess cheesecloth to form neat topknot.

3. Line each chilled serving plate with lettuce leaves, if desired. Place 6 clams on each plate. Garnish with lemon and pass a pepper mill.

Hamburgers Stuffed with Monterey Jack

6 ounces Monterey Jack cheese
1½ pounds freshly ground round steak
Freshly ground pepper
Sourdough or French bread
Salt
1 clove garlic, unpeeled and cut in half
Fresh spinach leaves for garnish, if grilling (optional)

If pan frying:
4 tablespoons olive oil
½ cup full-bodied red wine
2 tablespoons unsalted butter, at room temperature
1 tablespoon finely chopped fresh parsley

To grill:
1. Prepare fire. Place 4 dinner plates to warm in oven.
2. Grate cheese and shape into 4 slightly flattened balls, about the size of golf balls.
3. Divide ground beef into 4 portions. Handling as little and as gently as possible, press a ball of cheese into center of each portion, making sure cheese is surrounded by meat. You should have 4 large, slightly flattened patties.
4. Season on both sides with freshly ground pepper.
5. Cut bread at an angle into long, thick slices.
6. When fire is ready, toast sourdough on both sides and set aside. Place on heatproof platter and keep warm in oven.
7. Grill meat, turning with metal spatula once, until done to taste. Sprinkle with salt.
8. Just before meat is done, remove bread from oven and rub cut edge of unpeeled garlic clove over one side of each slice. Place one slice, garlic side up, on each plate. Top with spinach, if desired, and hamburger, and serve immediately, with additional toasted bread slices alongside.

To pan fry:
1. Grate cheese and shape patties as for grilling. Cut sourdough bread into long, thick slices.
2. Heat large skillet over medium-high heat.
3. Add 2 tablespoons olive oil, swirling to coat pan. Add sourdough slices and sauté quickly on both sides. Remove and rub one side of each slice with cut edge of the unpeeled garlic clove. Set on heatproof platter and keep warm in oven.
4. Heat remaining 2 tablespoons olive oil in pan. Add hamburgers and cook, turning once, until done to taste. Arrange hamburgers on the bread slices, sprinkle with salt, and keep warm in oven.
5. Pour off all fat from pan. Add red wine and reduce by

half. Remove pan from heat.

6. Just before serving, swirl butter and parsley into the reduced wine. Remove hamburgers from oven, spoon a small amount of sauce over each, and serve immediately.

Three-Bean Salad with Avocado

2 tablespoons red wine vinegar
1 tablespoon finely chopped fresh parsley
1 teaspoon chopped fresh oregano, basil, or coriander, or
   ½ teaspoon dried oregano
Salt and freshly ground pepper
½ cup olive oil
½ cup canned white kidney beans (also called cannellini)
½ cup canned red kidney beans
½ cup canned garbanzo beans (also called chick-peas)
½ cup canned golden hominy
1 small red onion
1 medium tomato
1 ripe avocado
1 tablespoon lime juice

1. Combine vinegar with herbs, salt, and pepper in bottom of salad bowl. Slowly drizzle in olive oil while stirring with fork.
2. Rinse the three kinds of beans in metal colander and the hominy in fine-meshed strainer under cold water to remove any canned taste. Drain thoroughly and add to the salad bowl. Toss with the vinaigrette to coat.
3. Peel red onion, and finely dice or thinly slice.
4. Core tomato and cut into small cubes.
5. Add onion and tomato to the bean and hominy mixture, and toss again. Let stand in cool place 10 to 15 minutes.
6. Just before serving, peel avocado and cut into cubes. Toss with lime juice in small bowl, then gently combine with the bean salad. Check seasonings and add salt and pepper, if necessary.

ADDED TOUCH

A sweet-onion marmalade makes a delectable relish or, when cooled, an alternative to the cheese stuffing for the hamburgers.

Onion Marmalade

2 pounds sweet onions
1 tablespoon olive oil
1 tablespoon sugar
1 teaspoon salt
Freshly ground black pepper
3 tablespoons red wine vinegar or sherry vinegar

1. Peel and dice onions. In heavy saucepan, heat oil and add onions, sugar, and salt and black pepper to taste.
2. Cover and cook over low heat, stirring from time to time, about 30 minutes.
3. Add wine vinegar. Cook over low heat, still covered, another 30 to 45 minutes, or until mixture is consistency of marmalade.

Susy Davidson

S usy Davidson, who comes from Oregon, is one of an adventurous new breed of American cooks who has specialized in classic French cooking techniques and then applied them to America's regional and ethnic recipes. Her solid French training has taught her the important skills that allow her to be both relaxed and creative with food. Like other cooks in this volume, she emphasizes using fresh ingredients, and she also creates unexpected combinations, such as the Chinese snow peas, the Italian fettuccine, and the American salmon of Menu 2.

Menus 1 and 2 give prominence to delicacies indigenous to the American Northwest, a region this cook predicts will be a "mecca for gastronomes," because of its vast array of fresh foods. One delicacy, the meaty, almost sweet Dungeness crab from her native Oregon, prompted her to invent the crab soufflé recipe of Menu 1, a light company luncheon or supper. She uses two unusual vegetables to accompany the soufflé: jicama, a crunchy tuber from Mexico popular in West Coast cooking, and Jerusalem artichokes, a vegetable that the colonists cultivated. Another Northwest specialty is Oregon's Columbia River salmon, which the cook had in mind when she devised her variation of stroganoff for Menu 2. Menu 3 calls for ingredients that have no particular American regional ties: pork chops, acorn squash, and red cabbage are popular nationwide. This makes a perfect fall dinner, when apples and acorn squash are best, but the ingredients are in the market all year.

A puffy, golden crab meat soufflé is the main dish for this light meal. Prepare the sunchoke and tomato salad and the green beans with jicama while the soufflé bakes. Serve the meal while the hot soufflé still holds its shape.

Crab Soufflé
Green Beans with Jicama
Sunchokes Vinaigrette

Fresh Oregon Dungeness crab is best for this recipe. However, you can certainly use the meat from fresh Maryland blue crab or Florida stone crab instead. Often the Oregon crab meat is flash frozen and then shipped to other parts of the country. If you use the frozen instead of the fresh, thaw it slowly, and take care to remove any bits of shell or membrane that may cling to the meat.

A soufflé is a dramatic baked dish that rises because of the air beaten into its egg whites. To make a soufflé that puffs up perfectly, have the egg whites at room temperature; then beat them with a pinch of salt until they are stiff and stand in peaks. At this point, fold them gently into the base, which in this recipe is a mixture of egg yolks, crab meat, scallions, and jicama. Although many cooks contend that you must beat egg whites in a copper bowl with a hand-held balloon whisk, you can use a perfectly clean stainless steel bowl and beat them with an electric mixer. Should you wish, you can add a pinch of cream of tartar to the whites before they become stiff to stabilize them and give them greater volume.

Both the soufflé and the green bean recipes call for jicama, a native Mexican vegetable shaped like a large turnip. Jicama has a taste and texture similar to that of water chestnuts, and is good raw or cooked. It is easy to find in West Coast supermarkets, but elsewhere, look for jicama at well-stocked greengrocers. This vegetable must be scrubbed well and peeled before using. Canned water chestnuts are an acceptable substitute in the soufflé.

The sunchoke, or Jerusalem artichoke, is a native American vegetable that is the knobby root of the perennial sunflower. Despite the name, the sunchoke is not related to the familiar green-leaved globe artichoke; yet when cooked to crisp-tender, the sunchoke tastes somewhat like an artichoke. Sunchokes are available all year in many supermarkets and health-food stores but are at their best in winter. Select firm chokes, and store them in a plastic bag in the refrigerator.

WHAT TO DRINK

The complex flavor of the crab soufflé needs a first-rate white wine, such as a Washington or New York State Riesling, a California Sauvignon Blanc or Fumé Blanc, or a good French Chablis.

SHOPPING LIST AND STAPLES

8 ounces fresh or frozen crab meat

1 small head Boston lettuce
1 pound sunchokes (also called Jerusalem artichokes)
1 medium-size jicama (about 1 pound), or 6-ounce can water chestnuts
¾ pound green beans (or 1½ pounds, if not using jicama)
4 to 6 cherry tomatoes or 1 large tomato (optional)
3 lemons
1 bunch scallions
1 bunch fresh chives
6 eggs
½ pint heavy cream
7 tablespoons unsalted butter
¼ pound Parmesan cheese
4 tablespoons safflower oil
2 tablespoons walnut oil
2 tablespoons white wine vinegar
2 teaspoons coarse-grain or Dijon mustard
2 teaspoons tomato paste
1½ teaspoons Worcestershire sauce
Dash hot pepper sauce
3 tablespoons flour
Salt and white pepper

UTENSILS

Large sauté pan or skillet
Large, heavy-gauge saucepan
Large saucepan
8-cup soufflé dish
Copper bowl (for soufflé, if using whisk)
2 large mixing bowls
Small bowl
Colander
Measuring cups and spoons
Chef's knife
Paring knife
Slotted spoon
Rubber spatula
Lemon zester
Vegetable scrub brush
Whisk or electric mixer

START-TO-FINISH STEPS

1. Squeeze lemon to measure 1 teaspoon lemon juice for crab soufflé. Reserve lemon for use in green beans recipe. Follow crab soufflé recipe steps 1 through 9.

2. Follow sunchokes vinaigrette recipe steps 1 through 3.
3. Bake soufflé, step 10.
4. Follow sunchokes vinaigrette recipe steps 4 and 5.
5. Follow green beans recipe steps 1 through 5.
6. Follow sunchokes vinaigrette recipe step 6, and serve with the green beans as soon as soufflé is done.

RECIPES

Crab Soufflé

6 small scallions
¼ pound jicama, or ½ cup canned water chestnuts
4 tablespoons unsalted butter
3 level tablespoons flour
¾ cup heavy cream
4 egg yolks
1 teaspoon coarse-grain or Dijon mustard
1½ teaspoons Worcestershire sauce
1 teaspoon lemon juice
Dash hot pepper sauce
2 teaspoons tomato paste
8 ounces fresh or frozen crab meat, finely flaked
Salt and white pepper
6 egg whites
1 to 2 tablespoons freshly grated Parmesan

1. Preheat oven to 375 degrees.
2. Chop scallions, using both white and green parts. You should have about ½ cup.
3. If using jicama, pare tough skin. Cut jicama or water chestnuts into ¼-inch dice to make ½ cup.
4. Melt butter in large, heavy-gauge saucepan. Sauté jicama or water chestnuts and scallions until scallions are soft, about 3 minutes.
5. Meanwhile, thoroughly butter 8-cup soufflé dish.
6. Sprinkle flour over the jicama and scallions. Cook, stirring, 1 minute. Add cream and stir until thickened. Do not let cream come to a boil.
7. Remove pan from heat and add egg yolks, one at a time, beating well after each addition. Add mustard, Worcestershire, lemon juice, hot pepper sauce, and tomato paste, and mix well. Stir in crab meat and season with salt and pepper to taste.
8. In large mixing bowl, preferably copper, whisk or beat egg whites with pinch of salt until firm but not dry. Lighten crab mixture by adding one quarter of the beaten egg whites and folding with rubber spatula to incorporate. Then, add crab mixture to the remaining egg whites and fold in gently.
9. Turn mixture into the buttered soufflé dish and set aside in area free from drafts until ready to bake.
10. Dust with grated Parmesan and bake about 25 minutes, until cooked through and well browned.

Green Beans with Jicama

¾ pound jicama
¾ pound green beans
Salt

1 small lemon
2 to 3 tablespoons unsalted butter

1. Peel jicama and cut into strips roughly the size of the green beans. Put into large saucepan filled with 1½ quarts cold, lightly salted water. Bring to a boil, cook 1 minute longer, and lift out with slotted spoon to drain in colander. Refresh immediately in cold water and drain again. Maintain water at a boil.
2. Meanwhile, wash beans thoroughly and snap off ends, pulling down to remove any strings.
3. Plunge beans into the boiling water used to cook the jicama. Cook until beans are crisp-tender, 3 to 4 minutes, depending on their size. Drain, refresh immediately in cold water, and drain again thoroughly.
4. Using zester, strip peel off lemon in long lengths. Be careful to avoid bitter white pith.
5. Melt butter in large sauté pan or skillet and sauté the beans and the jicama until heated through, about 5 minutes. Add salt to taste and the lemon zest, and toss. Transfer to serving bowl.

Note: If jicama is unavailable, you can double the quantity of green beans, using 1½ pounds total, and then proceed as recipe directs.

Sunchokes Vinaigrette

2 lemons
1 pound sunchokes (also called Jerusalem artichokes)
1 teaspoon coarse-grain or Dijon mustard
2 tablespoons white wine vinegar
2 tablespoons walnut oil
4 tablespoons safflower oil
Salt and white pepper
2 tablespoons chopped chives or scallion tops
Lettuce leaves
4 to 6 cherry tomatoes, halved, or 1 tomato, sliced, for garnish (optional)

1. In large saucepan bring 2 quarts lightly salted water to a boil. Squeeze in several tablespoons of lemon juice.
2. Scrub sunchokes. Trim tips of any protruding knobs and cut each sunchoke into ⅛-inch slices. Place slices in small bowl and sprinkle with lemon juice to prevent discoloration.
3. Blanch sunchoke slices in the boiling water until crisp-tender, about 5 minutes. Drain in colander, refresh immediately in cold water, and drain again thoroughly.
4. Meanwhile, combine mustard and vinegar in large mixing bowl. Add the oils in a slow, steady stream, whisking continually. Add chives or scallions and salt and pepper to taste.
5. When sunchokes are thoroughly drained and have cooled slightly, add them to the vinaigrette. Toss together and let stand until serving time.
6. Wash and dry lettuce leaves and line a serving platter with them. Place the sunchokes on the lettuce, draining off excess vinaigrette if necessary. Garnish with halved cherry tomatoes or tomato slices, if desired.

Salmon Stroganoff
Fettuccine with Dill Butter
Snow Peas and Cucumbers

A salmon stroganoff served on a bed of fettuccine and accompanied by snow peas and cucumber slices is a fine company dinner.

The classic stroganoff is a sauté of beef tenderloin served in a sauce thickened with sour cream. Susy Davidson's version uses salmon and heavy cream.

Crisp snow peas, also known as Chinese pea pods, combined with sliced cucumbers, are cooked quickly to retain crunch. If snow peas are not in season, double the cucumbers or use sugar snap peas.

The fresh fettuccine is seasoned with dill. If you cannot find fresh fettuccine, use a dried flat noodle, and follow package directions for cooking.

WHAT TO DRINK

This is a white-wine menu; a California Chardonnay or a fine French Burgundy would be perfect.

50

1 pound fresh salmon, boned and skinned
½ pound fresh mushrooms
½ pound snow peas or sugar snap peas
2 medium-size cucumbers
1 large onion
1 small bunch parsley
Fresh dill sprigs, or 1 teaspoon dried dill
1 pint heavy cream
1 stick plus 2 tablespoons unsalted butter
1 pound fresh egg fettuccine
3 tablespoons vegetable oil
1 teaspoon curry powder
Salt and white pepper
½ cup dry white wine

UTENSILS

Stockpot or kettle
12-inch skillet or sauté pan
Medium-size sauté pan
Large saucepan
Heavy-gauge medium-size saucepan
2 small plates
Small bowl
Colander
Measuring cups and spoons
Chef's knife
Paring knife
Slotted spoon
Vegetable peeler

START-TO-FINISH STEPS

1. Peel and slice onion for salmon recipe and follow steps 1 through 4.
2. Follow fettuccine recipe step 1 and snow peas recipe step 1. Chop fresh dill, if using, for the fettuccine.
3. Meanwhile, chop parsley for the salmon and follow salmon recipe step 5. Follow fettuccine recipe step 2.
4. Follow snow peas recipe steps 2 through 4.
5. Follow salmon recipe step 6, fettuccine recipe step 3, and snow peas recipe step 5. Serve at once.

RECIPES

Salmon Stroganoff

4 tablespoons unsalted butter
2 tablespoons vegetable oil
½ pound fresh mushrooms
Salt and white pepper
½ cup white wine
1 cup thinly sliced onion
1 teaspoon curry powder
2 cups heavy cream
1 pound fresh salmon, boned and skinned
¼ cup chopped fresh parsley

1. Melt 2 tablespoons of the butter with the oil in 12-inch skillet or sauté pan.
2. Wipe mushrooms and trim stem ends. Cut into thin slices. Sauté mushrooms in the butter and oil over medium heat about 5 minutes, stirring. Season to taste with salt and pepper. With slotted spoon remove the mushrooms to a small bowl.
3. Deglaze pan with white wine and allow to boil rapidly about 1 minute. Add remaining butter and sliced onion. Cook over medium heat until soft, about 5 minutes, stirring. Remove onions from pan and set aside on small plate.
4. Add curry powder and cook over low heat about 30 seconds. Pour in cream and bring to a gentle boil. Reduce volume by half; this will take about 20 minutes.
5. Slice salmon into ½-inch strips and set aside.
6. When cream is reduced, add the salmon strips and poach until tender, about 5 minutes. Add the mushrooms, onions, and parsley, and serve immediately.

Fettuccine with Dill Butter

4 tablespoons unsalted butter
1 tablespoon chopped fresh dill, or 1 teaspoon dried dill
1 pound fresh egg fettuccine

1. In large stockpot or kettle, bring 4 quarts of water to a boil.
2. In large saucepan, melt butter over low heat. Add dill.
3. Lightly salt the water, and cook the noodles until *al dente*, 2 to 3 minutes. Drain the noodles in colander and toss in the warm dill butter. Turn onto serving platter and top with Salmon Stroganoff.

Snow Peas and Cucumbers

2 medium-size cucumbers
½ pound snow peas or sugar snap peas
2 tablespoons unsalted butter
1 tablespoon oil
Salt and white pepper

1. In medium-size saucepan, bring 6 cups of lightly salted water to a boil.
2. Peel cucumber with vegetable peeler, leaving strips of the green peel for color. Halve cucumbers lengthwise, scoop out seeds, and cut each half into ⅛-inch slices.
3. Break off stem ends of snow peas and remove strings.
4. Blanch snow peas in the boiling water 1 minute; add the sliced cucumber and cook 1 more minute, until vegetables are crisp-tender. Drain in colander, refresh in cold water, and drain again thoroughly.
5. In medium-size sauté pan, melt butter with oil over medium heat. Toss the cucumbers and snow peas in the butter and oil, and heat thoroughly. Season to taste with salt and white pepper.

Pork Chops with Caramelized Apples
Acorn Squash with Pecans
Braised Red Cabbage

This imaginative fall meal, with apple flavors in two dishes and squash with nuts in a third, is sweet in character, but the sweetness is carefully controlled. The

This autumn meal lends itself to a rustic tablesetting and simple, homey serving pieces. Pork chops and sautéed apples arrive at the table with the squash and braised red cabbage.

main dish pairs pork with apples, a traditional Norman combination that French settlers probably brought to America. To intensify the apple flavor, Susy Davidson simmers the pork chops in fresh apple cider, an unadulterated blend of juices from pressed apples. You can also use pasteurized apple cider but not apple juice—the extra sugar added to it during processing makes it too sweet for this recipe. For the apple slices, choose a Golden

Delicious apple, which holds its shape well and does not discolor. You can also use a Baldwin, Empire, Macoun, or Northern Spy.

Although they cost a little extra, buy pre-shelled pecan halves for the squash because shelling pecans yourself takes time. If you wish, you can use pecan pieces instead; they are more economical than the halves. To prepare the squash for cooking, cut them in half lengthwise and scoop out pulp and seeds. To make them stable on the baking sheet, slice a thin piece off the bottom of each half, but take care not to cut too deeply. If acorn squash is not available, you can use butternut squash and handle it the same way.

WHAT TO DRINK

A soft red wine, particularly a Beaujolais, would be most

appropriate. Choose one from a single commune, rather than a plain Beaujolais. You could also get an interplay of flavors with a white Mâcon or similar dry white wine.

SHOPPING LIST AND STAPLES

4 center-cut pork chops, each about ¾ inch thick
2 acorn squash (about ½ pound each)
1 small head red cabbage (about 1 pound)
1 large Golden or Red Delicious apple
1 medium-size red onion
1 lemon
1 small bunch parsley
1 stick plus 4 tablespoons unsalted butter
2 tablespoons vegetable oil
¼ cup red wine vinegar
1½ cups fresh apple cider
1 tablespoon honey
1 to 1½ cups pecan halves
¼ teaspoon nutmeg
Salt
White pepper
¼ cup California Burgundy
¼ cup dry white wine

UTENSILS

10-inch skillet or sauté pan
Large, heavy-gauge saucepan with cover
Small saucepan
13-by-9-by-2-inch shallow baking dish
Heatproof platter
Medium-size bowl
Small bowl
Strainer
Measuring cups and spoons
Chef's knife
Paring knife
Metal turner
Wooden spoon
Tongs
Nutcracker (if using whole pecans)

START-TO-FINISH STEPS

1. Shell pecans, if necessary, and prepare acorn squash recipe steps 1 through 4. Juice lemon.

2. While squash is cooking, follow braised cabbage recipe steps 1 and 2.
3. Follow pork chop and apple recipe steps 1 through 6.
4. Follow braised cabbage recipe step 3, and serve with pork chops and squash.

RECIPES

Pork Chops with Caramelized Apples

2 tablespoons unsalted butter
2 tablespoons vegetable oil
4 center-cut pork chops, each about ¾ inch thick
¼ cup dry white wine
1¼ cups fresh apple cider
1 large Golden or Red Delicious apple
Juice of 1 lemon

1. Heat 1 tablespoon of the butter with the oil in large skillet or sauté pan. Brown chops 2 to 3 minutes on each side; remove to heatproof serving platter and cover loosely with foil.
2. Pour off excess fat and, using wooden spoon, deglaze pan with wine, scraping bottom of pan and stirring well. Add 1 cup of the apple cider and boil gently, stirring constantly, until wine-and-apple-cider liquid is reduced to 1 cup, about 5 minutes.
3. Meanwhile, peel, core, and cut apple in half lengthwise. With cut side down, slice each half into ⅛-inch slices. Put in medium-size bowl and sprinkle with lemon juice to prevent discoloration.
4. Return chops to pan and turn heat to low. Place the platter in oven to warm. Simmer chops until tender, about 10 minutes, turning them with tongs from time to time. Remove chops to the warm serving platter, cover loosely with foil, and keep warm.
5. Strain pan juices and reserve in small bowl. Add remaining ¼ cup cider and remaining butter, and heat until butter is melted. Add apple slices, being sure that each slice touches bottom of pan. Cook over medium-high heat, carefully turning apples once to coat them. Continue to cook until cider is reduced to a glaze and apple slices are caramelized but still hold their shape, about 10 minutes. Spoon apple slices onto the serving platter with the chops. Wipe out pan.
6. Return reserved juices to the pan and reduce to a light syrupy consistency. Spoon over the chops or serve in sauce boat.

Acorn Squash with Pecans

6 tablespoons unsalted butter
1 to 1½ cups pecan halves
2 acorn squash (about ½ pound each)
Salt and white pepper

1. Preheat oven to 375 degrees.
2. In small saucepan, melt butter. Add pecans and toss to coat.
3. Cut each squash in half and scoop out seeds and fibers. Generously season cavities with salt and pepper; then divide the pecan and butter mixture among them.
4. Place squash halves in large, shallow baking dish, fill bottom with 1 inch of water, and bake until squash is tender, about 40 minutes. Stir nuts from time to time while squash bakes to moisten them in the butter.

Braised Red Cabbage

4 tablespoons unsalted butter
1 medium-size red onion
1 small head red cabbage (about 1 pound)
¼ cup California Burgundy
¼ cup red wine vinegar
2 tablespoons apple cider
1 teaspoon salt
¼ teaspoon nutmeg
Dash white pepper
1 tablespoon honey
⅓ cup chopped fresh parsley

1. In large, heavy saucepan, melt butter. Chop onion coarsely. You should have about 1 cup. Cook the onion in the butter over medium heat until translucent, about 5 minutes.
2. Meanwhile, peel off and discard tough outer leaves of cabbage. Core cabbage and shred to make 6 cups. Add the cabbage to the cooked onion with the wine, vinegar, cider, salt, nutmeg, pepper, and honey. Stir to coat cabbage, cover, and cook over medium heat 20 minutes, if you prefer it a bit crisp, or 30 minutes, for a truer braise. Stir occasionally.
3. Toss with parsley just before serving.

ADDED TOUCHES

Indian pudding is probably a more traditional American dessert than apple pie, and there are as many versions of it as there are of chili con carne. In the past, the pudding was composed solely of cornmeal, molasses, milk, and spices, which were staples in the diets of poor country people. This is a slightly updated and delicious twentieth-century version. Begin preparation of this dish several hours before you plan to serve it.

Indian Pudding

½ cup yellow cornmeal
1½ cups cold milk or half-and-half
3 cups milk
4 tablespoons unsalted butter
¾ cup honey
1 teaspoon cinnamon
½ teaspoon ground ginger
½ teaspoon salt
3 eggs, lightly beaten
Vanilla ice cream or whipped cream (optional)

1. Moisten cornmeal with 1 cup of the cold milk or half-and-half. In medium-size heavy-gauge saucepan, scald the 3 cups of milk and add the cornmeal mixture. Cook over low heat, stirring constantly, until thickened and smooth, about 15 minutes.
2. Cover pan and continue to cook over low heat 30 minutes.
3. Preheat oven to 350 degrees.
4. Remove pan from heat and add butter, honey, cinnamon, ginger, salt, and eggs. Stir well to blend.
5. Pour pudding mixture into buttered 2-quart baking dish and pour remaining ½ cup cold milk or half-and-half over it. Bake until the custard is completely set, about 1½ hours.
6. Serve warm with vanilla ice cream or whipped cream.

Choose this simple, somewhat tart dessert for a light ending to the meal.

Strawberries with Sugar and Vinegar

1 quart fresh, ripe strawberries
½ cup superfine sugar, or to taste
1 teaspoon red wine vinegar
Grated zest of ½ lemon

1. Hull and slice strawberries.
2. Put strawberries in large serving bowl. Sprinkle with sugar and toss with red wine vinegar and zest. Let stand at least 1 hour before serving.

Richard Nelson

A merican cooking delights Richard Nelson; he thinks it is the best in the world. "American fare is plain fare that tastes wonderful," he says. He describes a classic American meal as fried chicken, mashed potatoes, and apple pie. Richard Nelson grew up on a ranch in South Dakota and ate basic food prepared by his grandmother—pancakes, fried eggs, cobblers, baking-powder biscuits, fried chicken, mashed potatoes, and apple pie. This childhood experience with home cooking shaped his food philosophy, one which should appeal to busy cooks today. He uses only readily available food, and he serves unpretentious meals. He prepares food simply, without heavy sauces and multiple seasonings to mask its taste, so that the flavor of the food stands on its own.

He lives in Oregon now, and the fresh provisions of the Northwest also influence his recipes. For instance, the main courses of Menus 1 and 3, the baked halibut and the venison chops, are indigenous to that part of the country. The butterflied leg of lamb in Menu 2 is lightly seasoned with rosemary butter and mustard, and is accompanied by two vegetable dishes—cauliflower fritters and a purée of peas and lima beans.

This informal family meal features ginger-flavored carrots and leeks, thick halibut steaks baked with a bread crumb topping, and a casserole of parslied rice. Flat-leaf parsley sets off the fish steaks effectively.

Baked Halibut
Gingered Carrots and Leeks
Green Rice Casserole

White-fleshed halibut, the main course for this non-seasonal family meal, has a delicate flavor. As with all fresh fish, select halibut steaks that have no aroma at all. The steaks marinate in buttermilk, salt, and pepper, and then get a bread crumb coating. If you wish, start marinating them in the morning. First pat them dry, then coat them with bread crumbs and add the mayonnaise and other ingredients to the baking pan. Refrigerate until you are ready to bake them in the evening. They cook very quickly, at high heat, a method that keeps them moist.

For the rice casserole with chopped parsley, use regular white rice rather than converted or instant rice, and rinse it only if the package is labeled "coated rice," which means the grains have been dusted with a powdered cereal and glucose for cosmetic reasons. For all other rice, rinsing is not only unnecessary; it also washes away valuable nutrients. You can keep cooked rice warm in a strainer over hot water, or in a covered pan in a low oven, for no longer than 30 minutes.

WHAT TO DRINK

The best accompaniment to this meal would be a crisp, dry white wine, well chilled. French Chablis, Pouilly Fumé, Sancerre, California Sauvignon Blanc, or New York Seyval Blanc are all possibilities.

SHOPPING LIST AND STAPLES

4 individual halibut steaks (about 4 to 6 ounces each)
6 carrots
2 leeks
1 onion
1 lemon (optional)
1 small bunch fresh parsley
1 clove garlic
Fresh ginger
1 stick plus 2 tablespoons unsalted butter
1 cup buttermilk
1 cup mayonnaise
2½ cups chicken stock, preferably homemade (see page 12), or canned
1 cup long-grain rice
4 slices day-old bread
1 teaspoon sugar
1 bay leaf

Paprika
Salt
Freshly ground pepper
2 tablespoons dry white wine

UTENSILS

Food processor or blender
2 medium-size saucepans with covers
2 small saucepans
13-by-9-by-2-inch baking dish
Shallow, nonaluminum dish
Small bowl
Measuring cups and spoons
Chef's knife
Paring knife
Rubber spatula
Vegetable peeler

START-TO-FINISH STEPS

1. Prepare and marinate halibut, step 1.
2. Trim and slice carrots and leeks, steps 1 and 2.
3. Process bread in blender or food processor to make about 1 cup bread crumbs for the halibut.
4. Mince onion and garlic, and chop parsley for the rice. Chop onion for the halibut.
5. Follow rice casserole recipe steps 1 through 4.
6. After halibut has marinated, follow steps 2 through 4.
7. Follow carrots and leeks recipe steps 3 through 5.
8. Follow halibut recipe step 5, carrots and leeks recipe step 6, and serve with rice.

RECIPES

Baked Halibut

1 cup buttermilk
Salt and freshly ground pepper
4 individual halibut steaks (about 4 to 6 ounces each)
1 cup fresh bread crumbs (approximately)
1 cup mayonnaise
2 tablespoons dry white wine
¼ cup chopped onion
Paprika
1 lemon, cut into 4 wedges for garnish (optional)

1. Combine buttermilk and salt and pepper to taste in shallow, nonaluminum dish and marinate fish 30 minutes.
2. Preheat oven to 500 degrees. Drain halibut thoroughly on paper towels. Wipe out dish.
3. Sprinkle bread crumbs in dish. Dip both sides of fish steaks in bread crumbs and arrange them side by side in greased shallow baking dish.
4. Combine mayonnaise, wine, and onion in small bowl and, with spatula, carefully spread evenly over the fish. Cover with thin layer of bread crumbs and dust with paprika. Bake 10 minutes, or until fish flakes easily when tested with fork.
5. Serve with lemon wedges, if desired.

Gingered Carrots and Leeks

6 carrots
2 leeks, white part only
1 stick unsalted butter
2 tablespoons minced fresh ginger
1 teaspoon sugar
1 teaspoon salt
½ teaspoon freshly ground pepper

1. Trim and peel carrots. Cut into thin strips.
2. Trim outer green leaves of leeks. Slice lengthwise to about 1 inch above root, slightly fanning leaves. Wash leeks thoroughly under cool running water to remove all sand and grit. Cut them into thin strips.
3. Melt 4 tablespoons of the butter in medium-size saucepan. Add 2 tablespoons cold water, ginger, sugar, salt, and pepper, and stir to dissolve the sugar.
4. Add the carrots and leeks, and stir to combine. Cover vegetables with foil, pressing the foil directly down on top of them. Cover saucepan. Cook over medium heat about 5 to 7 minutes, occasionally shaking pan.
5. Melt remaining 4 tablespoons of butter in small saucepan.
6. When vegetables are cooked, place in serving dish and pour melted butter over them.

Green Rice Casserole

2½ cups chicken stock
2 tablespoons unsalted butter
1 teaspoon minced onion
½ teaspoon minced garlic
1 cup long-grain rice
½ cup chopped fresh parsley
½ bay leaf

1. In small saucepan, bring chicken stock to a boil.
2. Melt butter in medium-size saucepan and add onion and garlic. Cook over low heat, stirring, until onion is soft.
3. Add rice, parsley, and bay leaf to the onion and garlic. Cook, stirring, about 2 minutes.
4. Add boiling stock to the rice mixture. Cover and simmer over low heat 20 minutes. Keep warm, if necessary (no more than 30 minutes). Discard bay leaf.

_____
ADDED TOUCH

Although this soufflé sounds complicated, you can assemble it in just a few moments and let it bake while you enjoy dinner. However, be sure to give the oven time to cool down after cooking the halibut. For the apricot pulp, Richard Nelson suggests using a 15-ounce can of apricot halves, drained and then puréed in a blender or food processor.

Apricot Soufflé

2 tablespoons unsalted butter
3 tablespoons unbleached all-purpose flour
¾ cup whole milk
2 teaspoons fresh lemon juice
1 cup cooked apricot pulp, or ½ cup apricot jam
5 egg yolks
4 tablespoons granulated sugar
6 egg whites, beaten stiff
Confectioners' sugar
Whipped cream for garnish (optional)

1. Reduce oven temperature to 350 degrees.
2. Butter 6-cup soufflé dish and add buttered collar (see diagram).

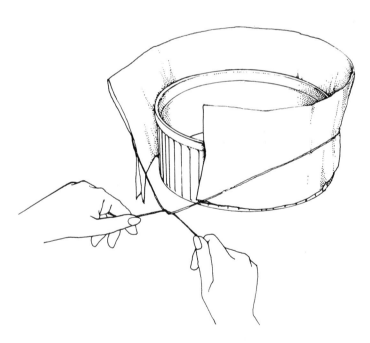

3. Melt butter in saucepan. Remove from heat and stir in flour. Return pan to heat, stir in milk, and cook, stirring, over medium heat until thick. Do not allow to boil. Add lemon juice and apricot pulp or jam. Mix in egg yolks, one at a time, and granulated sugar. Fold in egg whites.
4. Fill soufflé dish with the mixture. Bake 30 minutes.
5. Remove collar, dust soufflé with confectioners' sugar, and serve immediately. This is excellent with lightly whipped cream.

Broiled Leg of Lamb with Rosemary Butter and Dijon Mustard Sauce
Cauliflower Fritters
Purée of Peas and Lima Beans

Serve the lamb on a carving board; garnish the sauce with thin strips of orange peel, if you like.

Broiled butterflied leg of lamb, seasoned with rosemary butter and Dijon mustard, is an elegant main dish for a company meal. A "butterflied" leg means that the meat has been carefully cut off the bone in one large piece that resembles a large butterfly. Because deboning requires carving skill, ask your butcher to do this for you. Remember that some sections of the butterflied leg of lamb are thicker than others and cook more slowly. Broil the lamb 20 minutes on one side, 15 on the other. Then use a sharp knife to test for doneness in the thickest portion. If the meat is still pink and you prefer well-done lamb, broil it several minutes more.

WHAT TO DRINK

Despite the sweet-sharp sauce, the lamb and its accompaniments nevertheless need a fairly full-bodied red wine: a Margaux or similar wine from one of the other Bordeaux communes, a California Pinot Noir, or an Italian Dolcetto.

SHOPPING LIST AND STAPLES

5-pound leg of lamb, trimmed and butterflied
1 small head cauliflower
1 small bunch fresh rosemary

Fresh parsley sprigs (optional)
2 eggs
2 sticks unsalted butter
½ pint heavy cream
1 cup chicken stock, preferably homemade (see page 12), or canned
10-ounce package frozen peas
10-ounce package frozen lima beans
½ cup plus 2 tablespoons vegetable oil
3 tablespoons Dijon mustard
½ cup flour
Salt and freshly ground pepper

UTENSILS

Food processor (optional)
Large, heavy-gauge skillet
2 medium-size saucepans
Small saucepan
Broiler pan
Heatproof platter
Vegetable steamer
2 large mixing bowls
Small bowl
Colander
Strainer
Measuring cups and spoons
Long, thin-bladed knife for slicing meat
Paring knife
Slotted spoon
Long, double-pronged fork
Wire whisk
Food mill (if not using processor)

START-TO-FINISH STEPS

1. Follow lamb recipe steps 1 through 3.
2. Follow cauliflower recipe steps 1 and 2. In small bowl, beat eggs for fritters.
3. Follow puréed peas and lima beans recipe steps 1 and 2.
4. Follow cauliflower recipe step 3.
5. Make sauce for lamb, step 4.
6. When lamb is done, turn off oven and follow step 5.
7. Cook cauliflower fritters, steps 4 and 5.
8. Follow puréed peas and lima beans recipe step 3, remove fritters from oven, and serve with the lamb.

RECIPES

Broiled Leg of Lamb with Rosemary Butter and Dijon Mustard Sauce

5-pound leg of lamb, trimmed and butterflied
2 tablespoons vegetable oil (approximately)
2 tablespoons chopped fresh rosemary
Salt and freshly ground pepper
1 stick unsalted butter
3 tablespoons Dijon mustard

1. Preheat broiler.
2. Rub lamb all over with oil and 1 tablespoon of the rosemary. Sprinkle with salt and pepper.
3. Place lamb skin side up on broiler pan and broil 6 inches from heat source 20 minutes. Using long, double-pronged fork, turn lamb and broil another 15 minutes.
4. While lamb is broiling, melt butter with remaining rosemary in small saucepan and simmer a few minutes. Add mustard and remove from heat. Whisk until mustard is incorporated and mixture binds together.
5. When lamb is done, remove it to a carving board and let rest a few minutes. With long, thin-bladed slicing knife, cut at an angle into ¼-inch slices. Spoon sauce over the slices just before serving.

Cauliflower Fritters

1 small head cauliflower
½ cup flour
2 eggs, lightly beaten
½ cup vegetable oil
Salt and freshly ground pepper
4 tablespoons unsalted butter
1 tablespoon chopped fresh parsley for garnish (optional)

1. Trim cauliflower and cut into flowerets.
2. Steam cauliflower in vegetable steamer fitted in medium-size saucepan until tender, about 8 to 10 minutes. Drain in colander and put cauliflower through food mill, or purée in food processor.
3. In large mixing bowl, combine cauliflower with flour, eggs, 1 tablespoon of the vegetable oil, and salt and pepper to taste.
4. Heat large, heavy skillet and add remaining oil and butter. When hot, add batter to the fat by tablespoonfuls. Fry until golden brown on both sides, about 2 to 3 minutes. Remove with slotted spoon to a heatproof platter lined with paper towels. Repeat until all the batter is used.
5. Keep warm in oven until ready to serve. Garnish with parsley, if desired.

Purée of Peas and Lima Beans

10-ounce package frozen peas
10-ounce package frozen lima beans
1 cup chicken stock
3 tablespoons heavy cream
4 tablespoons unsalted butter, at room temperature
Salt and freshly ground pepper

1. Put frozen peas and lima beans in medium-size saucepan with chicken stock and cook over medium heat until lima beans are tender, about 5 to 7 minutes. Drain vegetables in strainer set over large bowl; reserve the stock.
2. Purée the drained vegetables in food processor, or put through food mill, adding heavy cream and butter. If vegetables seem too thick, add a bit more chicken stock. Do not add too much, or the purée will be too thin.
3. When ready to serve, reheat the purée in the saucepan and season to taste with salt and pepper.

Sautéed Venison Chops
Fresh Tomato Pudding
Belgian Endive with Vinaigrette Dressing

Venison chops, tomato pudding, and endive salad make an impressive autumn meal; red grapes and lettuce garnish each serving.

The special attraction of this autumn dinner is venison chops. Venison, the correct term for a butchered deer, is a seasonal meat available fresh only during hunting season in the fall. Nonhunters can buy venison from meat vendors who specialize in unusual varieties of meat, or they can ask a butcher to order venison chops. Unlike lamb chops, which have enough fat so that you can sauté them without extra oil, venison chops are dry and need fat during cooking. Hence, Richard Nelson adds butter to this recipe.

The tomato pudding tastes best when tomatoes are at their flavor peak. Select perfectly ripened tomatoes. To peel and seed them easily, lower whole tomatoes with a large slotted spoon into a pot of boiling water. Let them cook 30 seconds, remove them with the spoon, and allow them to cool 2 or 3 minutes. With a sharp paring knife, peel off the skin. It will come off easily. To seed the tomatoes, cut them in half crosswise and gently squeeze out the juice and seeds. What is left is the pulp, which you chop up for the pudding.

WHAT TO DRINK

Strong meats like venison should be accompanied by a robust red wine. Serve a good Bordeaux or a California Cabernet in the middle price range.

4 venison chops, each 1 inch thick
6 small tomatoes
2 heads Belgian endive
Watercress sprigs (optional)
1 orange (optional)
4 eggs
6 tablespoons unsalted butter
½ cup milk
¼ pound Parmesan cheese
4 slices white bread
2-ounce bottle onion juice
¼ cup olive or vegetable oil
1 tablespoon red wine vinegar
1¼ teaspoons sugar
Dash paprika
Salt and freshly ground pepper

UTENSILS

Large, heavy-gauge skillet
Medium-size saucepan
Small saucepan
1½-quart soufflé dish
2 large mixing bowls
Medium-size bowl
Small bowl
Measuring cups and spoons
Chef's knife
Paring knife
Slotted metal spoon
Rubber spatula
Metal turner or tongs
Wire whisk
Cheese grater

START-TO-FINISH STEPS

1. Grate Parmesan, separate eggs into 2 large mixing bowls, and follow tomato pudding recipe steps 1 through 5.
2. Follow endive salad recipe steps 1 and 2. Rinse and pat dry watercress, if using.
3. Ten minutes before pudding is done, cook venison chops, steps 1 and 2.
4. Dress salad, step 3, and serve with venison chops and tomato pudding.

RECIPES

Sautéed Venison Chops

4 tablespoons unsalted butter
4 venison chops, each 1 inch thick
Salt and freshly ground pepper

1. Melt butter in large, heavy-gauge skillet over high heat. When butter starts to brown, add chops but do not crowd them. Use 2 skillets if necessary.
2. Sprinkle with salt and pepper, and cook 3 to 4 minutes per side. Cook longer for well done—but remember that venison chops are best when served rare to medium rare. Serve immediately.

Fresh Tomato Pudding

6 small tomatoes
4 slices white bread, with crusts
½ cup milk
4 eggs, separated
2 tablespoons unsalted butter
1 teaspoon onion juice
1 teaspoon sugar
Salt and freshly ground pepper
Dash paprika
3 tablespoons grated Parmesan cheese plus additional cheese (optional)

1. Bring small pan of water to a boil. Add tomatoes and heat about 30 seconds. With slotted metal spoon, remove tomatoes, and peel, seed, and chop them.
2. In small bowl, soak bread in milk, and with a fork mash to a paste.
3. Preheat oven to 350 degrees. In 2 large mixing bowls, separately beat egg yolks and whisk or beat egg whites until stiff.
4. Melt butter in medium-size saucepan and add tomatoes, onion juice, sugar, and bread paste. Season to taste with salt and pepper, and add paprika. Remove from heat. Then incorporate grated Parmesan cheese and beaten egg yolks. Fold in egg whites.
5. Pour into buttered 1½-quart soufflé dish. Sprinkle additional Parmesan on top, if desired. Bake 35 minutes, or until pudding has risen and is set.

Belgian Endive with Vinaigrette Dressing

2 heads Belgian endive
¼ cup olive or vegetable oil
Salt and freshly ground pepper
1 tablespoon red wine vinegar
¼ teaspoon sugar
1 orange for garnish (optional)
Watercress sprigs for garnish (optional)

1. Halve and core endive. Wash the leaves thoroughly. Pat dry with cloth or paper towel, wrap in towel, and refrigerate.
2. Combine oil, salt, pepper, vinegar, and sugar in medium-size bowl, and mix well. Taste for seasonings and adjust if necessary.
3. When ready to serve, cut endive crosswise into 2-inch pieces and toss with the vinaigrette dressing to coat thoroughly. Peel orange and cut into thin slices. Serve on individual salad plates and garnish each salad with orange slices and watercress sprigs, if desired.

Miriam Ungerer

Food writer Miriam Ungerer, who lives on Long Island, New York, has never attended cooking classes nor had any formal restaurant experience. Instead, she has trained herself and has developed an individual style influenced primarily by the cooking of her native South Carolina, where seafood, rice, okra, fresh vegetables, and pungent spices are staples. To that foundation, she has added European, Oriental, and regional American techniques and dishes. Having lived and cooked in 10 different states, as well as in Europe, Miriam Ungerer has acquired a culinary education, but for the last decade, she has focused on preparing seasonal, all-American foods.

Her selection of menus highlights the delightful diversity of American cooking, from the Northeast to the Deep South to the Southwest. Southern cooking is the theme of Menu 1. The highly seasoned shrimp is a classic dish in South Carolina and once was served as a free snack at Carolina beach resorts. Country Captain, a curried chicken dish, is another Southern favorite.

Menu 2 features a traditional New England dish, deep-fried codfish balls, which were once a ritual for Sunday breakfast. Menu 3, a Southwestern meal, recalls Miriam Ungerer's years in San Antonio and balances the flavors used in the cooking of Mexican and German settlers in Texas. The mixed grill and coleslaw are dishes that San Antonians of German descent might serve, and the spicy black beans are seasoned with herbs and hot chilies often used in Mexican recipes.

For the first course, serve boiled shrimp in soup bowls and pass individual bowls of melted butter for dunking. This spicy company meal tastes best when the weather turns cool.

65

Hot Shrimp with Melted Butter
Country Captain
White Rice / Wilted Lettuce with Bacon

The first course here, hot shrimp simmered in beer, is a Carolinian dish and is seasoned not only by the beer but also by the onion and a blend of spices known as shrimp boil. This contains a secret combination of red pepper flakes, whole white peppercorns, bay leaf, celery seed, allspice berries, mustard seed, dill seed, coriander seed, ginger root, cinnamon stick, and whole cloves.

No one agrees whether Country Captain originated in Great Britain, the American South, or India. The main flavoring ingredient is curry powder. The commercial blends are usually mild and suitable for most curry dishes. For a more powerful curry flavor, increase the quantity of curry to taste. Before serving, garnish the chicken with sliced almonds, toasted ahead of time.

For foolproof rice to go with Country Captain, Miriam Ungerer suggests that you slip two sheets of paper towel between the pot and its lid; this absorbs excess moisture from the steaming rice and prevents it from becoming gummy.

WHAT TO DRINK

This menu builds on direct, vibrant flavors, so it needs a Zinfandel, which is fruity, full-bodied, and adaptable.

SHOPPING LIST AND STAPLES

1 frying chicken (2½ to 3 pounds)
1 pound medium-size shrimp (about 30)
4 thick strips bacon
1 head iceberg lettuce
1 large bell pepper
2 large onions
2 shallots
2 cloves garlic
1 bunch fresh parsley
1 stick plus 3 tablespoons unsalted butter
3 cups chicken stock, preferably homemade (see page 12), or canned (optional)
16-ounce can whole tomatoes
12½-ounce jar mango chutney (optional)
2 tablespoons bacon fat
2 tablespoons cider vinegar
1 teaspoon Dijon mustard
Hot pepper sauce
1½ cups long-grain rice
¼ cup sliced almonds

2 tablespoons black currants
1 tablespoon Old Bay shrimp boil
2 teaspoons curry powder (approximately)
½ teaspoon leaf thyme
Salt
Freshly ground black pepper
2 twelve-ounce bottles lager beer

UTENSILS

Large cast-iron skillet with heatproof cover
Medium-size skillet
Large saucepan with cover
Medium-size saucepan with cover
Small saucepan
Small baking pan
Medium-size bowl
Small bowl
Colander
Strainer
Measuring cups and spoons
Chef's knife
Paring knife
Wooden spatula
Tongs

START-TO-FINISH STEPS

1. Follow chicken recipe steps 1 through 3.
2. While chicken is browning, place almonds in baking pan and toast in oven, about 5 minutes, or until golden.
3. For the chicken, core and seed bell pepper, slice pepper and onion, and mince garlic. Drain tomatoes in strainer set over medium-size bowl and reserve their juice. Chop tomatoes.
4. Follow chicken recipe step 4.
5. Follow wilted lettuce recipe steps 1 and 2.
6. Peel and quarter onion, and follow shrimp recipe step 1.
7. Follow chicken recipe step 5.
8. Follow rice recipe steps 1 and 2.
9. Follow shrimp recipe steps 2 and 3.
10. Follow wilted lettuce recipe step 3.
11. Follow shrimp recipe step 4. While shrimp are cooking, chop shallots for wilted lettuce recipe.
12. Follow rice recipe step 3.
13. Follow shrimp recipe step 5 and serve.
14. A few minutes before chicken is ready, chop the fresh

parsley. Follow wilted lettuce recipe steps 4 and 5.

15. Remove chicken from oven, transfer to a serving platter, follow step 6, and bring to the table. Follow rice recipe step 4 and serve with wilted lettuce salad and chicken.

RECIPES

Hot Shrimp with Melted Butter

2 twelve-ounce bottles lager beer
1 tablespoon Old Bay shrimp boil
1 large onion, quartered
1 pound medium-size shrimp (about 30)
1 stick unsalted butter
Hot pepper sauce

1. In large saucepan, bring beer, shrimp boil, and onion to a simmer over medium-high heat. Cook 10 minutes.
2. Place shrimp in colander and rinse briefly under cold running water. Drain. Leave shrimp in their shells.
3. Melt butter in small saucepan over low heat and add a few dashes hot pepper sauce.
4. Add shrimp to the simmering beer, stir, and turn off heat. Cover and let sit 3 minutes.
5. Drain shrimp and put them in 4 individual serving bowls at the dining table. Provide small bowls for the shells and small cups of melted butter into which guests can dip their shrimp as they shell them.

Country Captain

1 frying chicken (2½ to 3 pounds)
2 tablespoons bacon fat
2 tablespoons unsalted butter
1 large onion, thinly sliced
1 large bell pepper, cut into thin strips
2 cloves garlic, minced
2 teaspoons curry powder, or more to taste
16-ounce can whole tomatoes, chopped
1½ teaspoons salt
1 teaspoon freshly ground black pepper
½ teaspoon leaf thyme, crushed
2 tablespoons black currants, rinsed
¼ cup toasted, sliced almonds
1½ tablespoons finely chopped fresh parsley
Mango chutney (optional)

1. Preheat oven to 350 degrees.
2. Disjoint, wash, and dry chicken. Split breast. (Save back, neck, wing tips, and giblets to make soup or stock.) Or, purchase chicken already disjointed.
3. Heat bacon fat in large cast-iron skillet and brown the chicken pieces. This will take about 10 minutes. Remove chicken with tongs and set aside on plate lined with paper towels.
4. If fat has darkened, rinse out skillet and wipe dry. Add butter, and when it melts, sauté the onion, bell pepper, garlic, and curry powder until the onion is soft. Add tomatoes and their juice, salt, pepper, and thyme. Simmer, uncovered, 10 minutes.

5. Return the chicken to the skillet and baste it well with the sauce. Remove skillet from heat, cover, and place in oven. Braise chicken about 30 minutes. During last 10 minutes of cooking, add currants and stir to combine. Do not overcook; a tender young fryer will disintegrate if cooked too long.
6. When ready to serve, sprinkle chicken with toasted almonds and chopped parsley. Serve with spicy mango chutney on the side, if desired.

White Rice

1 tablespoon unsalted butter
1½ cups long-grain rice
Salt
3 cups water or chicken stock
¼ cup chopped fresh parsley

1. Melt butter in medium-size saucepan. Add rice and sauté it over medium heat until well coated. Add pinch salt and water or stock, and bring to a quick boil.
2. Cover, lower heat to a bare simmer, and cook 15 minutes. Turn off heat.
3. Insert a piece of paper towel between the lid and the pan, and let sit at least 5 to 10 minutes. The rice can hold for up to an hour.
4. Toss with parsley just before serving with the chicken.

Wilted Lettuce with Bacon

1 head iceberg lettuce
4 thick strips bacon
1 tablespoon chopped shallots (about 2 whole shallots)
1 teaspoon Dijon mustard
2 tablespoons cider vinegar
Freshly ground black pepper

1. Trim wilted outer leaves or brown leaves from lettuce.
2. With chef's knife, shred lettuce as if you were making coleslaw; do not grate it, because you should have long, thin shreds. Put in salad bowl.
3. Slowly fry bacon in skillet, turning it often and taking care that the fat does not burn. Drain on paper towels.
4. Sauté shallots briefly in the bacon fat. Pour the shallots and hot bacon fat into small bowl and, with a fork, quickly beat in mustard, vinegar, and black pepper to taste. Immediately pour the hot dressing over the lettuce and toss well.
5. Crumble the reserved crisp bacon over the lettuce and serve at once.

LEFTOVER SUGGESTION

The Country Captain served with rice is such a delicious meal that you may wish to double the recipes for a second dinner that you can put on the table in just minutes. Save leftovers in covered containers in the refrigerator, and reheat them separately. To heat cold rice, put it in the top of a double boiler and cover it. You may add butter to keep the rice from sticking to the pan.

Deep-Fried Codfish Balls
Creamed Spinach
Pickled Beets with Herbs / Apricot Bread Pudding

Set one tray per person for the meal, and pass the sour cream separately. The apricot pudding cools while you eat.

There are many variations on codfish cake recipes, but two ingredients are always essential: shredded salt cod and mashed potatoes. Slabs of dried salt codfish were once staples in most New England pantries, but desalting and reconstituting this dried fish is time consuming, so Miriam Ungerer calls for using packaged codfish shreds, an old-fashioned product available in most supermarkets. The shreds need only minimal soaking, after which you can stir them right into the mashed potatoes. You can use leftover mashed potatoes for this recipe if they are very stiff; otherwise the codfish balls will fall apart as they cook. Leftover baked potatoes have the right texture and are particularly suitable for this recipe. Or, you can quickly make your own mashed potatoes. Start with 1¼ pounds of raw potatoes. Peel, cut up, and boil the potatoes until soft; then rice them or mash with a potato masher.

Vary the texture of creamed spinach as you prefer: purée it for a smooth consistency, or leave as is for more texture. Pickled beets with chopped scallions and parsley create a refreshingly tart counterpoint to the meal.

A custard-like apricot bread pudding concludes this family meal and is an essential part of the dinner. You can assemble the pudding quickly with items you probably have on hand. Miriam Ungerer suggests that you serve the pudding topped with whipped cream.

WHAT TO DRINK

This down-East, down-home menu would be good with beer or ale. If you prefer wine, choose a French Muscadet, a New York Seyval Blanc, or an Italian Soave or Pinot Grigio.

68

3 potatoes (about 1¼ pounds)
1 small bunch salad greens (optional)
1 bunch scallions
2 to 3 shallots, or 1 small white onion
1 small bunch fresh parsley
4 large eggs
3 cups milk, or 2 cups total, if using light cream for
    spinach
1 cup light cream
½ pint sour cream (optional)
7 tablespoons unsalted butter
16-ounce jar or 1-pound can pickled beets
2 ten-ounce packages frozen chopped spinach
2-ounce box Beardsley salt codfish shreds
2 cups vegetable or peanut oil
1 teaspoon vanilla extract
6 slices day-old home-style white bread
2 tablespoons flour
8-ounce package dried apricots
½ cup plus 1 tablespoon sugar
Freshly grated nutmeg
Freshly ground white pepper
Salt and freshly ground black pepper
2 ounces Cointreau or bourbon

UTENSILS

Food processor (optional)
Large, heavy-gauge saucepan
Medium-size heavy-gauge saucepan with cover
2 small saucepans
Deep-fry basket (optional)
11-by-17-inch cookie sheet
1½-quart soufflé dish or heatproof baking dish
4 medium-size bowls
Fine-meshed strainer
Measuring cups and spoons
Chef's knife
Paring knife
Slotted metal spoon or Chinese mesh spoon
Wooden spoon
Wire whisk
Ricer or potato masher
Scissors
Deep-fat thermometer

Vegetable peeler (optional)
Nutmeg grater

START-TO-FINISH STEPS

The night before, or at least 1 hour before: Refrigerate the pickled beets, step 1.

1. Peel and cut up potatoes for codfish. Boil in water to cover until tender.
2. Follow apricot bread pudding recipe steps 1 through 6.
3. When potatoes are tender, drain and put through ricer, or mash with potato masher in bowl.
4. Follow creamed spinach recipe step 1.
5. Chop parsley and scallions, and follow codfish recipe steps 1 and 2.
6. Follow creamed spinach recipe steps 2 through 5. Remove pudding from oven, step 7, and turn off oven.
7. Remove beets from refrigerator and follow step 2. Complete codfish recipe, steps 3 through 5, and serve at once with spinach and beets. For dessert, serve apricot bread pudding.

RECIPES

Deep-Fried Codfish Balls

2-ounce box Beardsley salt codfish shreds
2 cups mashed potatoes (about 1¼ pounds cooked)
1 large egg
½ teaspoon freshly ground black pepper
Dash freshly grated nutmeg
2 tablespoons finely minced parsley
2 tablespoons finely minced scallions, with some green
Salt (optional)
2 cups vegetable or peanut oil

1. Empty codfish into bowl and add 1½ cups cool water. Wait 30 seconds, squeeze dry, and add to the bowl of mashed potatoes. Empty bowl and wipe dry.
2. Combine egg, pepper, nutmeg, parsley, and scallions in the dried bowl. Add the codfish and potato mixture. Taste for salt. (You may not need any; codfish is quite salty.)
3. Heat oil in large, heavy-gauge saucepan until it reaches 390 degrees on deep-fat thermometer or until it browns a scallion ring in about 30 seconds. If you have a simple, old-fashioned fry basket, put it in the oil. Otherwise, have on hand a slotted metal spoon or a Chinese mesh spoon.
4. When oil is ready, use a table fork to take up clumps of

codfish mixture and gently ease them into the hot oil. Work quickly and do not overcrowd pan. They will be crisp, spiky, and brown in 2 to 3 minutes.

5. Drain on cookie sheet lined with paper towels and keep warm in turned-off oven while you cook remaining codfish balls. Serve hot.

Creamed Spinach

2 ten-ounce packages frozen chopped spinach
½ teaspoon salt
3 tablespoons unsalted butter
2 to 3 shallots, or 1 small white onion, minced
2 tablespoons flour
1 cup milk or light cream
Salt and freshly ground white pepper
Dash freshly grated nutmeg

1. Bring 2 cups of water to a boil in medium-size heavy-gauge saucepan and add frozen spinach and ½ teaspoon salt. Cover; break up with a fork as soon as the spinach softens. Simmer 5 minutes and drain in fine-meshed strainer. Wipe out saucepan.

2. Melt butter in the saucepan and stir in shallots or onion. Cook over low heat until transparent. Add flour and cook, stirring, about 3 minutes. Meanwhile, bring milk or cream to a boil in small saucepan.

3. Off heat, add the boiling milk or cream to the roux and beat well with whisk to avoid lumping. Return pan to low heat.

4. Squeeze excess liquid out of spinach with your hands and add to the béchamel sauce. Season to taste with salt, pepper, and nutmeg.

5. You may serve spinach as is, or purée it in food processor, which will give a smooth, satiny texture. Cover spinach to keep warm until ready to serve.

Pickled Beets with Herbs

16-ounce jar or 1-pound can pickled beets
3 to 4 scallions, chopped
Fresh parsley sprigs, chopped
Freshly ground black pepper
¼ cup sour cream for garnish (optional)
Salad greens for garnish (optional)

1. In medium-size bowl, chill beets overnight or at least 1 hour before serving.

2. When ready to serve, toss with scallions, parsley, and

pepper. Top each serving with dollop of sour cream and serve on a bed of greens, if desired.

Apricot Bread Pudding

⅔ cup dried apricots
6 slices day-old home-style white bread
4 tablespoons unsalted butter, softened
2 cups milk
3 large eggs
½ cup plus 1 tablespoon sugar
2 ounces Cointreau or bourbon
1 teaspoon vanilla extract

1. Preheat oven to 350 degrees. With scissors, snip dried apricots into ½-inch pieces.

2. Trim crusts and butter each bread slice thickly. Cut slices into uniform cubes.

3. Butter 1½-quart soufflé dish or heatproof baking dish. Add bread cubes and apricots and stir.

4. In small saucepan, heat milk to scalding.

5. In medium-size bowl, beat eggs well with ½ cup sugar and pour the scalded milk over them, whisking constantly. Whisk in Cointreau and vanilla. Pour over the bread and apricot mixture, and sprinkle top with remaining tablespoon of sugar.

6. Bake in center of oven 30 to 40 minutes, until puffy and lightly browned.

7. Remove from oven and cool 15 minutes before serving.

LEFTOVER SUGGESTIONS

Because of their concentrated natural sugars, dried apricots make a sweet, nutritious snack to eat right from the box. Another way to use up leftover dried apricots is to poach them in water to cover with sugar to taste and a few drops of almond extract. Cook 15 minutes or until they are tender. You serve them warm for breakfast or topped with whipped cream for dessert. To make an apricot glaze for tarts or coffee cakes, simmer the apricots in sugar and water until they reduce to a thick, mushy consistency, then purée them.

Cook a double batch of the creamed spinach; there are a number of ways you can use it as part of a light lunch or supper. Thin it with chicken stock and heat gently for a delicious soup.

Mixed Grill / Spicy Black Beans
Coleslaw with Caraway Vinaigrette
Sliced Tomatoes and Red Onions

Fresh daisies and simple pottery arranged on a patterned cloth make an effective backdrop for this barbecue. Serve the grilled meats and tomato-onion salad on dinner plates, and the cole-slaw and spicy beans as side dishes.

The German-style mixed grill and the spicy south-of-the-border black beans are an ideal summer barbecue. You baste the chicken wings before and during grilling with a soy-based marinade. Before cooking, season the lamb kidneys with salt, pepper, and mustard; the bratwurst cooks without any added seasoning. Bratwurst, a German pork sausage seasoned with herbs, is readily available in most supermarkets. A sausage commonly substituted for bratwurst is weisswurst, a delicately flavored light veal sausage, also a German product. When you grill, keep a bulb baster and a jar of water handy to put out any flames caused by the fat dripping onto the coals.

The black beans, fiery with dried chilies and also flavored with cumin, coriander, garlic, and onion, are a Mexican-style dish. If you have the time, you may prefer to start with dried beans rather than canned ones. If so, the cook suggests soaking 1 pound of black beans in water to cover overnight in a large pot. Next day, drain the beans and cover them again with fresh water. The beans will require about 2 hours' simmering time until they become soft. When they are about three quarters cooked, add 1 tablespoon Kosher salt plus all other ingredients except the bacon.

For the coleslaw with caraway seeds, select a firm, compact head of green cabbage. Core it and discard any wilted leaves. Cut the head into quarters. To shred, use a large, sharp knife or a Chinese cleaver and slice through the quarters lengthwise. Allow the shreds to marinate in the vinaigrette. Do not chill or the olive oil will solidify.

WHAT TO DRINK

Among the best possibilities for this dinner are a California Fumé Blanc or a Sauvignon Blanc, or a French white from the Rhône—a white Châteauneuf-du-Pape would be excellent. Good dark beer or ale would also be good.

SHOPPING LIST AND STAPLES

8 chicken wings
4 bratwurst, or other all-pork sausage
4 whole lamb kidneys
2 thick strips bacon
1 small head green cabbage
3 large vine-ripened tomatoes
2 small red onions

1 large yellow onion
3 cloves garlic
Fresh ginger
4 tablespoons unsalted butter
2 pounds canned black beans (also known as turtle beans), or 1 pound dried
8-ounce can tomato sauce
3 tablespoons olive oil
1 tablespoon red wine vinegar
2 tablespoons prepared mustard (approximately)
2 teaspoons honey
2 tablespoons soy sauce
2 dried chili peppers
1 bay leaf
1 tablespoon ground cumin
1 tablespoon ground coriander
1 tablespoon caraway seeds
1 tablespoon Kosher salt
Salt and freshly ground pepper

UTENSILS

Outdoor grill
Food processor or blender
Large skillet with heatproof cover
Small saucepan
3 small bowls
Colander
Measuring cups and spoons
Light Chinese cleaver (optional)
Chef's knife
Paring knife
Tongs
Wire whisk
Basting brush or bulb baster
Poultry pins or bamboo skewers

START-TO-FINISH STEPS

If using dried black beans, prepare in advance: Soak overnight. The next day, drain and cook in fresh water to cover 2 hours. After 1½ hours, add 1 tablespoon Kosher salt and cook another 20 to 30 minutes. At this point, the beans are ready to be combined with remaining ingredients.

1. Make charcoal fire or start gas grill for mixed grill recipe, step 1. With flat side of chef's knife, mash garlic clove to a pulp and mash ginger to make 1 teaspoon for mixed grill.

2. Follow black beans recipe steps 1 and 2. Mince garlic, chop onion, and continue with recipe, steps 3 through 6. If using bamboo skewers for mixed grill, soak them in water to cover in sink.

3. While beans are cooking, follow mixed grill recipe steps 2 through 4.

4. Follow coleslaw recipe steps 1 and 2.

5. Follow mixed grill recipe step 5. While kidneys are grilling, slice tomatoes and red onions.

6. Follow black beans recipe step 7 and serve with the mixed grill, coleslaw, and tomatoes.

RECIPES

Mixed Grill

2 tablespoons soy sauce
4 tablespoons unsalted butter
2 tablespoons prepared mustard (approximately)
1 clove garlic, mashed to a pulp
1 teaspoon mashed fresh ginger
2 teaspoons honey
8 chicken wings
4 bratwurst, or other all-pork sausage
4 whole lamb kidneys
Salt and freshly ground pepper

1. Build charcoal fire and let it burn at least 30 minutes. Or start fire for gas grill.

2. Melt butter in small saucepan over low heat. With fork, beat together soy sauce, 1 teaspoon prepared mustard, garlic, ginger, and honey in small bowl until well combined. Brush or baste chicken wings with the marinade and place them on grill.

3. At the same time, put bratwurst on to grill. Using tongs, turn and baste chicken wings frequently; they should be cooked and nicely crisped in about 20 minutes. The bratwurst, too, should be turned frequently; it will also cook in about 20 minutes.

4. Split lamb kidneys without cutting all the way through. Thread each kidney crosswise on poultry pin or bamboo skewer so that it lies flat. If you are using bamboo skewers, first soak them in water so they will not burn. Season kidneys with salt and lots of pepper, and brush with prepared mustard.

5. About 6 minutes before chicken and bratwurst are cooked, add kidneys to grill and brush with the melted butter. Cook about 3 minutes per side, brushing with butter when you turn them. Divide mixed grill among 4 dinner plates and serve.

Spicy Black Beans

2 dried chili peppers
2 thick strips bacon
2 cloves garlic, minced
1 large yellow onion, chopped
1 tablespoon ground cumin
1 tablespoon ground coriander
1 bay leaf
8-ounce can tomato sauce
½ cup hot water
2 pounds canned black beans (also known as turtle beans), or 1 pound dried black beans, cooked
Salt

1. Wash chilies thoroughly and split them open. Handle carefully: the juice can burn if it gets near your eyes or lips, so it is wise to rinse your hands after handling chilies. Discard seeds and stems, and tear the chilies into pieces. In small bowl, cover them with boiling water and let soak 10 minutes.
2. Fry bacon slowly in skillet until crisp. Drain on paper towels. Do not pour off bacon fat.
3. Sauté garlic and onions in the bacon fat until transparent. Stir in cumin and coriander and cook a few minutes.
4. Add bay leaf, tomato sauce, and water, and blend well.
5. Drain beans in colander and rinse with warm water. Add to the sauce and stir to combine.
6. Purée the chilies in blender or food processor with some of their soaking liquid and add them to the beans. Cover and cook on top of stove about 30 minutes to blend flavors. Or you may cook them in a 350-degree oven 30 minutes.
7. Turn black beans into a heavy serving bowl. Crumble the reserved bacon over the top at serving time.

Coleslaw with Caraway Vinaigrette

1 small head green cabbage
1 tablespoon Kosher salt
1 tablespoon red wine vinegar
3 tablespoons olive oil
1 teaspoon prepared mustard

Freshly ground pepper
1 tablespoon caraway seeds

1. Core and slice cabbage into fine shreds. (A light Chinese cleaver is the ideal tool for this.) Place in serving bowl and sprinkle with the salt.
2. In small bowl, whisk together vinegar, oil, mustard, and a generous amount of pepper. Pour this dressing on the cabbage and stir in caraway seeds. Let stand at room temperature until ready to serve. This coleslaw should not be chilled.

Sliced Tomatoes and Red Onions

3 large vine-ripened tomatoes
2 small red onions

Slice tomatoes and onions, and arrange them on serving platter. Fresh local tomatoes are splendid and need no frills; they should be served plain, except for the onions.

ADDED TOUCH

A dessert of fresh fruit mixed with walnuts is a refreshing conclusion to this barbecue. The basis for the compote is a ripe pineapple, split in half, cut into small triangles, and peeled. You can mix any seasonal fruit—such as blueberries, peaches, strawberries, or blackberries—with the pineapple chunks.

Pineapple, Banana, and Walnut Compote

1 fresh, ripe pineapple
2 small ripe bananas
¼ cup coarsely chopped walnut meats
Splash of rum or bourbon

1. Split pineapple in half lengthwise and cut flesh into small triangles. Trim tough skin. Place in serving bowl. Slice banana into rounds and immediately mix with pineapple. This prevents discoloration of the bananas.
2. Add walnuts and rum, stir to combine, and chill.

LEFTOVER SUGGESTION

Use any leftover black beans to make a hearty soup. Simply purée the beans, with chicken stock, in a blender or food processor.

Ann Seranne

A nn Seranne began her cooking career in an American college laboratory, studying food chemistry and learning about cooking at a molecular level. This meticulous training has given her an uncluttered approach to devising recipes. She has a simple formula for successful home cooking: use fresh, wholesome ingredients and eliminate fussy preparation. Her philosophy explains why she has been well known to generations of American cooks.

This prolific cookbook writer, food columnist, and early proponent of the kitchen blender says that, among other things, American cooking has become very sophisticated and Americans have become very interested in exotic foods. An increasingly popular ethnic style of cooking is the Tex-Mex food of the Southwest, which she highlights in Menu 1. This is an informal meal, consisting of a creamy chick-pea soup and a Rio Grande salad, which is made from flour tortillas that have been fried into cup shapes, and then filled with lettuce, chili, tomatoes, avocados, and black olives.

By contrast, the other two menus call for ingredients that are standard throughout the country and available all year long. The simple-to-prepare entrée of Menu 2, fillets of flounder, are rolled up jelly-roll fashion and then poached. They are served with a fresh mushroom salad. The entrée of Menu 3 is an uncomplicated poultry recipe, with a fresh vegetable on the side.

This Tex-Mex meal of chick-pea soup and Rio Grande salad is ideal for a buffet lunch or dinner. You can serve the main course salad in tortilla cups, or set out the cups, filled only with shredded lettuce and chili, and let your guests sprinkle on their own taco toppings to taste. Pass the salad dressing in a small pitcher.

Spicy Chick-Pea Soup
Rio Grande Salad with Buttermilk Dressing

This Southwestern menu provides a festive meal, and if you double the recipes, it would be enough for a buffet. Chick-peas, or garbanzo beans, are a particularly popular legume in the Southwest. In this recipe, cumin gives the chick-pea soup its Mexican flavor. If you have the time, you may prefer to reconstitute dried garbanzo beans, sold packaged in supermarkets, rather than use the canned beans. (The advantage is that you can thus control the salt content.) To do this, rinse the dried beans, then soak them overnight in a large container in four parts water to one part beans. The next day, pour off the soaking water and replace it with fresh water, three parts water to one part beans. Bring the beans to a slow boil and simmer them until tender, 2 to 3 hours.

The Rio Grande salad features flour tortillas, made from wheat flour rather than cornmeal. You will find fresh flour tortillas in the dairy case of most supermarkets. Ann Seranne prefers to use the very large 12-inch round tortillas, but the smaller 8-inch and 10-inch tortillas are acceptable and usually easier to find.

WHAT TO DRINK

First choice for this menu is a dark Mexican beer or a dark ale. If you prefer wine, choose a fruity, full-bodied red, such as a California Gamay or young Zinfandel, a French Côtes du Rhône, or an Italian Barbera or Dolcetto.

SHOPPING LIST AND STAPLES

1 pound extra-lean ground round
2 large bunches scallions
1 head iceberg lettuce
1 ripe California avocado
1 large ripe tomato, or ½ pint cherry tomatoes
1 lemon
1 small onion
1 clove garlic
Fresh parsley sprigs
½ cup buttermilk
½ pint light cream
1 tablespoon unsalted butter
¼ pound white Cheddar cheese
20-ounce can chick-peas
2 cups chicken stock, preferably homemade (see page 12), or canned
½ cup pitted black olives
1 package flour tortillas, 10 to 12 inches in diameter

1 cup, plus 1 tablespoon (optional), vegetable or peanut oil
2 tablespoons salad oil
1 tablespoon red wine vinegar
½ cup mayonnaise
4 tablespoons flour
3 tablespoons chili powder
1½ teaspoons ground cumin
1 teaspoon oregano
½ teaspoon dry mustard
¼ teaspoon paprika
Dash Cayenne pepper
Salt and freshly ground pepper

UTENSILS

Large, heavy-gauge skillet
Medium-size skillet
Medium-size saucepan
11-by-17-inch cookie sheet
Small bowl
Measuring cups and spoons
Chef's knife
Paring knife
Tongs
Cheese grater
Whisk
Deep-fat thermometer
Soup ladle

START-TO-FINISH STEPS

1. Follow salad recipe steps 1 and 2.
2. Prepare buttermilk dressing.
3. Preheat oven to 200 degrees.
4. Prepare accompaniments for salad: shred lettuce, chop scallions, shred cheese, chop tomatoes and black olives, and peel, pit, and coarsely chop avocado.
5. Follow chick-pea soup recipe steps 1 through 3.
6. Fry the tortillas for salad, step 3.
7. Follow soup recipe step 4, salad recipe step 4, and serve everything at once.

RECIPES

Spicy Chick-Pea Soup

6 scallions
20-ounce can chick-peas with liquid

1 tablespoon unsalted butter
2 tablespoons flour
2 cups chicken stock
½ teaspoon ground cumin
Dash Cayenne pepper
Salt and freshly ground pepper
½ cup light cream
1 tablespoon red wine vinegar

1. Trim and wash scallions. Slice white portions and crisp parts of the green stalks. Mince 4 teaspoons of the green tops and set aside for garnish.
2. Set aside 4 tablespoons of the chick-peas for garnish.
3. Heat butter in medium-size saucepan and sauté the sliced scallions 2 minutes. Stir in flour and blend well. Gradually stir in stock. Add chick-peas with their liquid and cook, stirring, until thickened. Add cumin, Cayenne, and salt and pepper to taste. Gently boil 10 minutes, stirring occasionally.
4. Just before serving, stir in cream and vinegar. Reheat and ladle into soup bowls. Garnish each serving with the reserved minced scallion greens and chick-peas.

Rio Grande Salad with Buttermilk Dressing

1 pound extra-lean ground round
1 tablespoon vegetable or peanut oil (optional)
2 tablespoons flour
3 tablespoons chili powder
1 teaspoon each crumbled oregano, ground cumin, and minced garlic
1 cup hot or boiling water
Salt
1 cup vegetable or peanut oil (approximately)
4 to 8 flour tortillas, 10 to 12 inches in diameter
1 head iceberg lettuce, shredded (about 4 cups)
4 or 5 scallions, chopped (about ½ cup)
¼ pound white Cheddar cheese, shredded (about 1 cup)
Buttermilk dressing (see following recipe)
½ cup chopped ripe tomato or quartered cherry tomatoes
½ cup chopped pitted black olives
1 ripe California avocado, peeled, pitted, and coarsely chopped

1. In medium-size skillet, cook beef over medium heat until it loses all red color, adding 1 tablespoon vegetable oil to skillet, if necessary, to prevent sticking. Sprinkle with flour, chili powder, oregano, cumin, and garlic, and cook 1 minute. Stir in water and salt to taste.
2. Simmer chili over low heat, covered, stirring occasionally; add a little more water, if needed, to keep moist.
3. Fill large, heavy-gauge skillet to a depth of 1 inch with vegetable or peanut oil and heat over medium-high heat until deep-fat thermometer registers 360 degrees. Using kitchen tongs, place a tortilla in the hot fat and let it bubble 30 seconds. While it is bubbling, press soup ladle against the tortilla, using tongs to mold the tortilla to the bowl of the soup ladle (see diagrams). With tongs, crimp edges of the tortilla to make them fluted. Fry until lightly brown on one side, about 1 minute. Remove ladle and, using tongs, turn tortilla. Cook 30 seconds longer, or until brown. Drain on cookie sheet lined with paper towels. Keep warm in preheated oven while cooking remaining tortillas.
4. To assemble salad, place fluted tortillas on dinner plates and cover bottoms generously with shredded lettuce. Top lettuce with some chili, sprinkle with scallions and Cheddar cheese, and top with several spoonfuls of buttermilk dressing. Sprinkle with diced tomatoes, chopped black olives, and avocado.

Buttermilk Dressing

½ teaspoon dry mustard
¼ teaspoon paprika
1 teaspoon chopped onion
¼ teaspoon freshly ground pepper
¼ teaspoon chopped garlic
1 tablespoon chopped parsley
1 tablespoon lemon juice
2 tablespoons salad oil
½ cup mayonnaise
½ cup buttermilk

Combine all ingredients in small bowl, whisking or beating with a fork until smooth. Refrigerate until serving time.

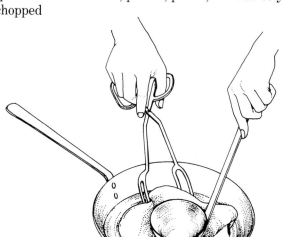
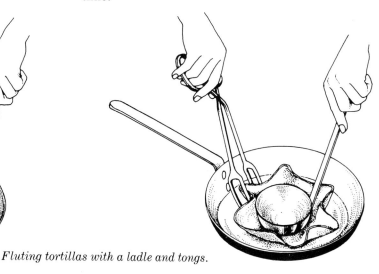

Fluting tortillas with a ladle and tongs.

Fillets of Flounder Capri
Lemon Rice
Mushroom Salad

Rolled fish fillets with a saffron-tinted sauce look like company fare but are easy to assemble. Pass the salad of sliced mushrooms, celery, and scallions, and the bowl of rice, garnished with lemon rind, when you serve the fish.

Fresh flounder or sole fillets are the focal point of this light, uncomplicated meal. Flounder is a moderately priced flatfish with a delicate, sweet flesh. Some members of the flounder family are called sole—the lemon sole and the gray sole, for example—but the only genuine sole comes from Europe. In coastal area fishmarkets, fresh flounder is usually sold in fillets but sometimes is sold whole. If this is the case, ask your fishmonger to fillet the whole fish for you. Away from the coasts, most flounder are sold as frozen fillets. To prepare the fillets for cooking, curl them jelly-roll fashion; then arrange them in a skillet filled with bubbling poaching liquid: dry white wine, clam juice, or chicken stock and seasonings. When removing the cooked fish rolls from the skillet, handle them carefully because they are fragile and can break apart easily.

Cream and butter both thicken and enrich the stock, the wine makes it fragrant, and saffron adds both color and flavor. The world's costliest spice, saffron is available ground but most often as whole threads. A little goes a long way. A quarter ounce should last for many months of cooking. Saffron is easy to find in the spice section of most supermarkets and in specialty food shops.

The fresh mushroom salad, with diced celery and scallions, is dressed with a basic wine vinegar and olive oil vinaigrette, spiked with a sprinkling of dry mustard.

WHAT TO DRINK

Buy a good, crisp Italian white—a Pinot Grigio or Pinot Bianco. You could also serve a fully dry California Chenin Blanc or a Seyval Blanc from New York State.

SHOPPING LIST AND STAPLES

4 fillets of flounder or gray or lemon sole (about 1½ pounds total weight)
¾ pound fresh mushrooms
1 large ripe tomato
1 small bunch scallions
3 celery stalks
1 small bunch fresh parsley
1 lemon
1 clove garlic
½ pint heavy cream
1 stick plus 3 tablespoons unsalted butter

8-ounce bottle clam juice or ⅓ cup chicken stock, preferably homemade (see page 12), or canned
⅓ cup olive oil
3 tablespoons white wine vinegar
1 cup rice
¼ teaspoon crushed thread saffron or 1 teaspoon Dijon
  mustard
1 teaspoon dry mustard
1 small bay leaf
Freshly ground white pepper
Salt
Freshly ground black pepper
⅓ cup dry white wine or dry vermouth

UTENSILS

10-inch skillet
Medium-size saucepan with tight-fitting cover
Small saucepan
Heatproof serving platter
Medium-size serving bowl
Small bowl
Measuring cups and spoons
Chef's knife
Paring knife
Wooden spoon
Slotted spoon

START-TO-FINISH STEPS

1. Chop celery and scallions for mushroom salad, and
follow steps 1 and 2.
2. Cook rice, steps 1 and 2, and chop parsley. Mince garlic
and chop parsley for flounder recipe.
3. Bring 1 cup of water to a boil in small saucepan; add
tomato for flounder recipe, and blanch 30 seconds. Using
slotted spoon, remove tomato and peel, seed, and chop.
4. Follow flounder recipe steps 1 through 3.
5. Follow rice recipe step 3.
6. Follow flounder recipe step 4.
7. Follow rice recipe step 4, remove mushroom salad from
refrigerator, and serve everything at once.

RECIPES

Fillets of Flounder Capri

4 fillets of flounder or gray or lemon sole (about 1½
  pounds total weight)
3 tablespoons unsalted butter
⅓ cup clam juice or chicken stock
⅓ cup dry white wine or dry vermouth
¼ teaspoon minced garlic
¼ teaspoon crushed thread saffron or 1 teaspoon Dijon
  mustard
1 small bay leaf
1 tablespoon chopped parsley

1 large ripe tomato, peeled, seeded, and chopped (about
  1 cup)
Freshly ground white pepper
Salt (optional)
½ cup heavy cream

1. Wipe fillets with damp paper towels. Cut in half lengthwise, discarding any line of tiny bones that may run down
center of fish. Roll each half, starting with widest portion,
into a plump little jelly roll. Preheat oven to 200 degrees.
2. Rub bottom of 10-inch skillet with 2 tablespoons of the
butter. Add broth, white wine or vermouth, garlic, saffron, bay leaf, parsley, tomato, and pepper. Bring to a boil.
Arrange fish rolls, standing them on end, in the sauce and
simmer about 6 minutes, basting occasionally.
3. Using slotted spoon, transfer fish rolls to heatproof
serving platter and keep warm in oven.
4. Taste sauce and add salt, if needed. Add cream and
gently simmer over medium heat, stirring constantly with
wooden spoon, about 3 minutes, or until sauce thickens
and coats the spoon. Remove skillet from heat and swirl in
remaining tablespoon of butter. Pour the sauce over the
fish.

Lemon Rice

1 cup rice
1½ cups water
¼ teaspoon salt
1 lemon
1 stick unsalted butter
2 tablespoons chopped parsley

1. In medium-size saucepan with tight-fitting cover, bring
rice, water, and salt to a rapid boil. Reduce heat to very
low, cover saucepan tightly, and cook 20 minutes, or until
rice is done.
2. While rice is cooking, remove rind from lemon in long
strips and squeeze juice into small bowl.
3. In small saucepan, melt butter. Cut lemon rind into
slivers. Add rind to the melted butter and sauté 3 minutes.
4. Add butter to the cooked rice. You may discard the rind
or not, as desired. Toss rice with lemon juice and chopped
parsley before turning into serving bowl or spooning onto
individual dinner plates.

Mushroom Salad

¾ pound fresh mushrooms
1 cup chopped celery
3 tablespoons chopped scallions
1 teaspoon dry mustard
Salt to taste
Freshly ground black pepper
3 tablespoons white wine vinegar
⅓ cup olive oil

1. Wipe mushrooms with dampened paper towels and
trim off any hard stem ends. Slice mushrooms thinly.
2. Combine all ingredients in serving bowl and marinate
in refrigerator 30 minutes, or until time to serve.

Smoked Salmon with Capers
Tarragon-Broiled Game Hens
Braised Celery / Flamed Peaches

While the game hens broil, offer the smoked salmon. Bring the peaches to table in a bowl; then transfer them to a skillet to flambé.

Smoked salmon is an elegant first course. Purchase top-quality salmon and have it sliced paper thin. Since salmon is quite perishable, refrigerate and use it quickly.

The plump Rock Cornish game hens are split, then broiled. To split them and open them, you will need a well-sharpened chef's knife and a smaller boning knife to remove each backbone and breastbone.

WHAT TO DRINK

Choose a California Chardonnay or Sauvignon Blanc, a white Burgundy or a good Graves, or an Italian Gavi.

SHOPPING LIST AND STAPLES

2 Rock Cornish game hens (about 1½ pounds each)
8 thin slices smoked salmon (about ½ pound total)
2 large bunches celery
4 fresh ripe peaches
2 lemons
1 clove garlic
1 small bunch fresh parsley
1 small bunch fresh tarragon, or 1 tablespoon dried
1 small bunch watercress
1 stick plus 2 tablespoons unsalted butter

¼ pound Parmesan cheese
1½ cups chicken stock (approximately), preferably home-
    made (see page 12), or canned
3½-ounce bottle capers
1 cup granulated sugar
1 tablespoon vanilla extract
Kosher salt and freshly ground black pepper
Freshly ground white pepper
⅓ cup brandy, kirsch, or rum
1 tablespoon peach liqueur or apple brandy

UTENSILS

12-inch skillet with tight-fitting cover
Large saucepan
Broiler pan with rack
Chafing dish or heatproof skillet
Small bowl
Measuring cups and spoons
Chef's knife
Paring knife
Metal spoon
Wooden spoon
Tongs
Cheese grater
Basting brush

START-TO-FINISH STEPS

1. Follow braised celery recipe steps 1 through 3.
2. Squeeze lemon half to measure 1 tablespoon juice,
mince garlic clove, and chop fresh tarragon, if using.
Prepare game hens and follow steps 1 through 4.
3. Cut 1½ lemons into wedges, rinse watercress and pat
dry, and prepare salmon appetizer. Serve.
4. Peel, halve, and pit peaches. Follow flamed peaches
recipe steps 1 through 3.
5. Grate Parmesan with cheese grater and follow celery
recipe steps 4 and 5.
6. Follow game hens recipe step 5 and serve with celery.
7. For dessert, flame the peaches, step 4, and serve.

RECIPES

Smoked Salmon with Capers

8 thin slices smoked salmon (about ½ pound total weight)
1 small bunch watercress
Lemon wedges
4 teaspoons drained capers

Roll salmon into "rosettes" and place on serving platter
lined with watercress. Garnish with lemon wedges and
sprinkle each rosette with ½ teaspoon capers.

Tarragon-Broiled Game Hens

2 Rock Cornish game hens (about 1½ pounds each)
1 stick unsalted butter, at room temperature
1 tablespoon lemon juice

1 teaspoon minced garlic
3 tablespoons chopped fresh tarragon, or 1 tablespoon
    dried
½ teaspoon Kosher salt, crumbled
Freshly ground black pepper
2 tablespoons chopped fresh parsley

1. Preheat broiler.
2. Split game hens down back and flatten with hand.
3. In small bowl, cream butter with lemon juice, garlic,
and tarragon. Brush both sides of hens with some of the
creamed butter and arrange hens on broiler rack, skin
side down. Sprinkle with salt and pepper.
4. Place broiler rack about 4 inches below heat source.
Broil hens, brushing every 5 minutes with the butter
mixture, 15 minutes. Use tongs to turn chicken and brush
with more butter. Broil another 10 to 15 minutes.
5. Sprinkle with parsley; serve one half to each person.

Braised Celery

2 large bunches celery
1½ cups chicken stock (approximately)
Freshly ground white pepper
Salt
2 tablespoons unsalted butter
¼ cup freshly grated Parmesan cheese

1. Trim coarse outer stalks from celery and reserve for
another purpose. Cut both bunches in half lengthwise,
through the inner hearts and surrounding tender stalks.
Arrange cut side up in large skillet.
2. Add enough chicken stock to barely cover the celery.
Sprinkle generously with freshly ground pepper and a
little salt, and dot with butter.
3. Bring stock to a boil, cover skillet tightly, and braise
over low heat 35 to 40 minutes.
4. When celery is easily pierced with a fork, set aside until
ready to serve. It will keep warm in the braising liquid.
5. Using tongs, carefully remove celery. Serve half a heart
to each person, along with a little of the savory juice.
Sprinkle generously with grated cheese.

Flamed Peaches

4 fresh ripe peaches
1 cup granulated sugar
1 tablespoon vanilla extract
⅓ cup (scant 3 ounces) brandy, kirsch, or rum
1 tablespoon (½ ounce) peach liqueur or apple brandy

1. Peel, halve, and pit peaches. In large saucepan, combine 1 cup water, sugar, and vanilla. Bring to a boil and boil
rapidly 5 minutes.
2. Add peaches; poach 6 to 8 minutes, turning once.
3. Using metal spoon, transfer peach halves to heatproof
skillet or chafing dish with a little of the hot syrup.
4. Pour brandy and peach liqueur over peaches; ignite. If
peaches and syrup have cooled, warm brandy before pouring it over peaches. Serve flaming, if desired.

Beverly Cox

MENU 1 (Left)
Cajun-Style Shrimp Stew
Steamed Rice
Tossed Green Salad with
Sherry Vinegar Dressing

MENU 2
Endive, Watercress, and Beet Salad
Pork Chops with Yam and Sausage Stuffing
Steamed Broccoli Flowerets
Tart Applesauce

MENU 3
Fresh Asparagus Soup
Rack of Lamb with Fresh Mint Sauce
Tomatoes Stuffed with Herbed Rice

Food writer and cookbook author Beverly Cox studied classical cooking techniques in France and brings her strong French training to bear on American recipes, which are now a major interest of hers. Her challenge is to adapt classic French dishes and techniques to American foodstuffs. She uses wholesome ingredients in easy-to-prepare recipes, a trend more and more American cooks are following.

The entrées here are American, but you can recognize the French connection. For instance, the Cajun-style shrimp stew is a purely American meal, but Cajun cooking was nonetheless created by Acadian (hence the nickname "Cajun") settlers in backwoods Louisiana. Cajun cooking is a conglomerate of French Canadian, American Indian, and black cooking traditions. Another French touch is pork, in its many forms a staple of Norman cookery, but Americanized here in a recipe that features a savory stuffing of yams, raisins, sausage meat, and onions.

As a food stylist, Beverly Cox pays close attention to the details that create a beautiful meal. Whether it be for family or guests, she believes that the visual impact of a meal is as important as its taste, as these three menus demonstrate. The rosy-hued Cajun-style shrimp stew of Menu 1 contrasts with the white rice and the greens of the salad. The rack of lamb of Menu 3, with paper frills on the ribs, is beautifully composed on its platter. The colors and textures of the foods in Menu 2 are carefully balanced to provide a harmonious presentation.

In this table setting, dinnerware with a shell motif sets off the Cajun shrimp stew, garnished with parsley, served on a bed of rice, and accompanied by a green salad.

Cajun-Style Shrimp Stew
Steamed Rice
Tossed Green Salad with Sherry Vinegar Dressing

This Cajun menu teaches two useful and basically simple techniques: making a roux and using shrimp shells to make a flavorful stock. A roux is a paste, made from melted fat and flour, that thickens sauces and gravies. In the classic French roux, the paste is cooked until the flour turns golden-brown and loses any raw taste. The Cajun black roux cooks longer, about 15 to 20 minutes, and takes some patience to produce. You must add the flour slowly and stir the paste carefully over low heat until it thickens and turns a deep chocolate brown. The slow cooking produces a clean, powerful taste. Beverly Cox warns you not to hasten the browning process by turning up the heat, because you will burn the roux.

While you are preparing the roux, let the shrimp-shell broth simmer and reduce, and cook the rice in a covered pot. You can assemble the shrimp recipe very quickly once the roux and the broth are ready. Have the onion, garlic, and diced pepper handy to stir into the roux. You can easily fix this three-step dish in an hour by having all the ingredients ready before you start to cook.

The tossed green salad contains two different leafy greens and sliced fresh fennel, which tastes like anise and looks rather like celery, with a bulb at its bottom and feathery leaves at the top. Select a pale greenish-white bulb and avoid any that are discolored, soft, or cracked.

If you would like to serve a first course, try a ham and melon combination. Buy a small, ripe cantaloupe and twelve paper-thin slices (about 6 ounces) of Smithfield ham or prosciutto. Chill the cantaloupe, then cut it in half and scoop out the seeds. Cut each half into six wedges and remove the rind. Arrange melon wedges and loosely rolled slices of ham on a serving platter, and garnish with lime wedges.

WHAT TO DRINK

This Louisiana-style dinner calls for a good, chilled white wine, one with a bit of spiciness. A dry Riesling or Gewürztraminer, from California or Alsace, would be ideal. If you want a softer wine with a suggestion of sweetness, try a German Kabinett from the Moselle or Rheingau. Cold lager beer would also be enjoyable.

SHOPPING LIST AND STAPLES

1½ pounds fresh medium-size shrimp
2 to 3 heads Bibb or Boston lettuce, depending on size
½ small head curly chicory or escarole
1 medium-size cucumber or 1 bulb fresh fennel
1 green bell pepper
1 bunch fresh parsley
1 large white or yellow onion
1 clove garlic
1 cup long-grain rice
⅓ cup peanut or olive oil
¼ cup vegetable oil and/or bacon drippings
4½ teaspoons sherry vinegar, or 1 tablespoon white wine vinegar and 1½ teaspoons dry sherry
5 tablespoons all-purpose flour
¾ teaspoon Dijon mustard
2 tablespoons Worcestershire sauce
1½ teaspoons hot pepper sauce
1 bay leaf
Salt and freshly ground pepper

UTENSILS

Large, heavy-gauge skillet
2 medium-size saucepans with covers
Large bowl
Small bowl
Colander
Mesh sieve
Measuring cups and spoons
Chef's knife
Paring knife
Wooden spatula
Whisk
Cheesecloth
Salad spinner (optional)

START-TO-FINISH STEPS

1. Follow shrimp stew recipe steps 1 through 3.
2. Follow salad recipe steps 1 through 3.
3. Follow stew recipe step 4.
4. While roux is cooking, prepare rice.
5. Mince onion and garlic, dice green pepper, and follow stew recipe steps 5 through 7.
6. While stew is simmering, make salad dressing and assemble salad, steps 4 and 5.
7. Follow shrimp stew recipe step 8 and serve with rice and salad.

Cajun-Style Shrimp Stew

1½ pounds fresh medium-size shrimp
3½ cups water
4 or 5 fresh parsley sprigs
1 bay leaf
Salt
¼ cup vegetable oil and/or bacon drippings
5 tablespoons all-purpose flour
1 cup finely diced onion
1 clove garlic, minced
¼ cup diced green bell pepper
2 tablespoons Worcestershire sauce
1½ teaspoons hot pepper sauce
¼ cup minced fresh parsley

1. Rinse and shell shrimp.
2. Place shrimp shells, water, parsley sprigs, bay leaf, and ½ teaspoon salt in medium-size saucepan and bring to a boil over high heat. Reduce heat to medium and simmer 8 to 10 minutes, or until liquid is reduced to about 2½ cups.
3. While broth is simmering, devein shrimp. Set aside.
4. To make Cajun black roux, place oil and/or bacon drippings and flour in large, heavy-gauge skillet and cook over medium heat, stirring constantly, 15 minutes, or until mixture turns a rich chocolate color. When gauging the color of the roux, remember that when you add liquid, the sauce will lighten a shade or two.
5. When roux has attained the proper color, add onion and garlic, and stir constantly over moderate heat 3 minutes. Add diced pepper and continue to cook and stir 2 minutes more.
6. Strain shrimp broth through mesh sieve lined with double layer of cheesecloth.
7. Gradually add the strained broth to the roux and bring to a boil, stirring until the sauce is smooth. Season with Worcestershire, hot pepper sauce, and about 1 teaspoon salt. Simmer 8 to 10 minutes.
8. When ready to serve, stir shrimp into the simmering mixture and cook until just firm, 2 to 3 minutes. Sprinkle with minced parsley and serve over rice.

Tossed Green Salad with Sherry Vinegar Dressing

2 to 3 heads Bibb or Boston lettuce, depending on size
½ small head curly chicory or escarole
1 medium-size cucumber or 1 bulb fresh fennel
4½ teaspoons sherry vinegar, or 1 tablespoon white wine vinegar and 1½ teaspoons dry sherry
¾ teaspoon Dijon mustard
1½ teaspoons minced fresh parsley
⅓ cup peanut or olive oil
Salt and freshly ground pepper

1. Rinse greens thoroughly in colander under cold running water and dry in salad spinner or pat dry with paper towels.
2. Trim, rinse, and slice cucumber, but do not peel unless waxed. You will need about ¾ cup. If using fennel, rinse, trim, and slice thinly. Reserve feathery fennel leaves for garnish.
3. Reserve 8 whole leaves of lettuce for garnish. Tear remaining greens into bite-size pieces and place in large bowl with sliced cucumber or fennel.
4. In small bowl, combine vinegar, mustard, and parsley. Add oil in a slow stream, beating constantly with whisk or fork. Add salt and pepper to taste, and beat again briefly.
5. Line sides of salad bowl with slightly overlapping lettuce leaves. When ready to serve, toss the greens and cucumber or fennel with the dressing and mound in center of salad bowl. Garnish with the reserved fennel leaves, if using.

Steamed Rice

2 cups water
1 cup long-grain rice
1 teaspoon salt

In medium-size saucepan, bring water to a boil over high heat. Stir in rice and salt; cover. Lower heat and cook 15 to 20 minutes, or until all the liquid is absorbed. Keep warm, covered, until ready to serve with shrimp.

ADDED TOUCH

You should prepare this lightly spiced custard the morning you plan to serve it, or even the night before, so that it can cool and set.

Louisiana Honey Custard

2 eggs plus 2 egg yolks
4 tablespoons light-colored honey
¾ teaspoon vanilla extract
2 cups milk
Nutmeg and mace, or cinnamon

1. Preheat oven to 375 degrees.
2. Place whole eggs, yolks, honey, and vanilla in large mixing bowl and whisk until yellow and frothy.
3. In medium-size saucepan, heat milk to just below boiling point and add to the egg mixture in a steady stream, whisking constantly.
4. Pour custard through wire mesh strainer into 4 heatproof custard cups or ramekins.
5. Skim any foam off top of custard to assure a smooth surface. Sprinkle lightly with nutmeg and mace or with cinnamon.
6. Place custard cups in heatproof baking dish with sides at least 2½ inches high. Place baking dish on middle rack of preheated oven. Carefully pour enough boiling water into the dish to reach halfway up sides of the custard cups.
7. Reduce heat to 350 degrees and bake 30 minutes, or until custard is set. Do not let water around custard come to a boil or custard will overcook and be grainy.
8. Serve custard chilled or at room temperature.

Endive, Watercress, and Beet Salad
Pork Chops with Yam and Sausage Stuffing
Steamed Broccoli Flowerets / Tart Applesauce

Pork chops, stuffed with a yam and sausage mixture, and broccoli flowerets are an impressive arrangement on a serving plate. Pass the applesauce and the endive-watercress salad separately.

These loin pork chops—stuffed with yams, raisins, diced onion, sausage, and herbs—are a delicious Southern dish. To cut a pocket in the chops for stuffing, make an inch-long incision at the middle of the boneless side with a sharp knife, moving the blade back and forth to widen the interior pocket. Withdraw the knife, then insert your finger to stretch and ready the pocket for stuffing. There are two types of sweet potatoes—the larger, orange one, called a yam, and the smaller, yellowish sweet potato—and they are interchangeable in recipes. The chestnut-like flavor of cooked sweet potato is enhanced by the seasonings here and the sweet wine, Madeira.

For the Belgian endive, watercress, and pickled beet salad, select creamy white endive with firm crisp heads. The watercress should be very fresh, with crisp stems and bright green leaves.

For a tart, full-flavored applesauce, make your own. Beverly Cox recommends Granny Smith, Rome Beauty, Northern Spy, or, possibly, McIntosh apples. To give your sauce a delicate pink tinge and to enhance the flavor, cook the apples unpeeled, then strain before serving. Be sure to taste the sauce before deciding whether you need to add the optional honey. The applesauce should be very tart, to offset the sweet and spicy richness of the pork chop stuffing.

WHAT TO DRINK

The delicate vegetable flavors in this menu require a light red wine, such as a California Gamay, a French Beaujolais, or a simple Chianti. A substantial white wine would also do: for instance, a moderately priced California or New York Chardonnay.

SHOPPING LIST AND STAPLES

4 loin pork chops, each 1 inch thick, with pockets cut for stuffing
¼ pound spicy bulk pork breakfast sausage
1 bunch broccoli (about 1½ pounds)
2 tart cooking apples (about ½ to ¾ pound total weight)
1 yam or sweet potato (about ¼ pound)
1 onion
1 to 2 heads Belgian endive
1 bunch watercress
1 small bunch fresh parsley
1 shallot or scallion
1 lemon

5 tablespoons unsalted butter
16-ounce jar sliced pickled beets
1 tablespoon golden raisins (optional)
½ cup beef stock
1 cup unsweetened apple cider or juice
⅓ cup safflower or peanut oil
3 tablespoons cooking oil
4 teaspoons red wine vinegar
2½ teaspoons Dijon mustard
1 teaspoon honey (optional)
Dash ground thyme
Dash Cayenne pepper
Salt
Freshly ground pepper
3 tablespoons Madeira wine

UTENSILS

Food processor (optional)
Large, heavy-gauge skillet with heatproof handle and
    cover
Medium-size sauté pan
2 medium-size saucepans with covers
Small, heavy-bottomed saucepan
Vegetable steamer
Large plate
2 large mixing bowls
Medium-size mixing bowl
Small bowl
Colander
Measuring cups and spoons
Chef's knife
Paring knife
Slotted metal spoon
Wooden spatula
Rubber spatula
Whisk
Tongs
Ricer or potato masher
Lemon zester
Toothpicks
Apple corer (optional)
Salad spinner (optional)

START-TO-FINISH STEPS

1. Dice onion, mince parsley, and follow stuffed pork chops recipe steps 1 through 8.
2. Follow salad recipe step 1.
3. Peel, core, and quarter apples. Prepare applesauce, step 1.
4. Mince shallot or scallion and parsley, and follow salad recipe steps 2 and 3. Follow applesauce recipe step 2.
5. Follow broccoli recipe steps 1 and 2.
6. Follow salad recipe step 4.
7. Remove pork chops from oven, step 9.
8. Follow broccoli recipe steps 3 and 4, and bring to the

table with the salad and applesauce.
9. Finish pork chops recipe, step 10, and serve at once.

RECIPES

Endive, Watercress, and Beet Salad

1 to 2 heads Belgian endive
1 bunch watercress
1 cup sliced pickled beets, well drained
1 teaspoon finely minced shallot or scallion
4 teaspoons finely minced fresh parsley
1½ teaspoons Dijon mustard
4 teaspoons red wine vinegar
⅓ cup safflower or peanut oil
Salt
Freshly ground pepper

1. Trim endive and cut leaves lengthwise into spears ½ inch wide. Trim watercress stems. Rinse greens under cold running water and dry in salad spinner or pat dry with paper towels or a kitchen towel. Refrigerate, wrapped in a towel, until needed.
2. Place beets in medium-size mixing bowl.
3. In small bowl, combine shallot, 2 teaspoons of the parsley, mustard, and vinegar. Add oil in a slow stream, whisking constantly, until oil is incorporated. Add salt and pepper to taste.
4. Arrange endive spears in a fan on each salad plate. Remove watercress from refrigerator. Toss beets and watercress with the vinaigrette and arrange on top of the fanned endive. Sprinkle with remaining minced parsley and serve as a first course.

Pork Chops with Yam and Sausage Stuffing

1 yam or sweet potato (about ¼ pound)
3 tablespoons unsalted butter
2 tablespoons diced onion
¼ pound spicy bulk pork breakfast sausage
Dash ground thyme
Salt
Freshly ground pepper
Dash Cayenne pepper
1 tablespoon minced parsley
1 tablespoon golden raisins (optional)
4 loin pork chops, 1 inch thick, with pockets cut for
    stuffing
3 tablespoons cooking oil
3 tablespoons Madeira
½ cup beef stock
1 teaspoon Dijon mustard

1. In medium-size saucepan, bring 2 cups water to a boil.
2. Peel and cube yam, and boil 3 minutes, or until barely tender. Then rice or mash it and turn into large mixing bowl.
3. Melt 1 tablespoon of the butter in large, heavy-gauge skillet. Add onion, crumble in sausage, and sauté 8 to 10

minutes over medium heat, stirring constantly, until onion is translucent and sausage is cooked through and lightly browned.

4. Using slotted metal spoon, transfer onion and sausage to the mixing bowl. Add ½ teaspoon salt, ¼ teaspoon pepper, Cayenne, parsley, and raisins; toss together until thoroughly combined.

5. Stuff pockets of pork chops until they are moderately full and close them with crisscrossed toothpicks. Wipe out skillet.

6. Preheat oven to 325 degrees.

7. Heat oil in the skillet. When oil is hot, brown pork chops on both sides, using tongs to turn them, about 4 minutes on each side. Transfer them to large plate and sprinkle lightly with salt and pepper.

8. Pour off oil in skillet. Add remaining 2 tablespoons of butter and heat. Return chops to the skillet and pour 1 tablespoon of the Madeira over them. Cover and cook until the meat is sizzling. Then set the covered skillet in lower third of oven and cook 25 to 30 minutes. Turn and baste the chops once or twice during cooking.

9. Remove skillet from oven. Arrange pork chops on platter and cover loosely with foil.

10. Skim as much fat as possible from pan juices and discard fat. Return skillet to top of stove, add beef stock, remaining 2 tablespoons of Madeira, and mustard, and boil rapidly over high heat, scraping bottom of skillet to incorporate all the browned bits into the sauce. Boil 2 to 3 minutes, or until sauce has reduced to about ½ cup. Spoon sauce over the pork chops and serve immediately.

Steamed Broccoli Flowerets

1 bunch broccoli (about 1½ pounds)
2 tablespoons unsalted butter
Salt and pepper

1. In medium-size saucepan fitted with a vegetable steamer, bring water to a boil.

2. Divide broccoli into flowerets with 2- to 3-inch stems. (Reserve remaining stems for soup or another use.)

3. Steam broccoli, covered, until barely tender, 2 to 3 minutes. Drain in colander. Plunge broccoli into large bowl of cold water for a few seconds to stop the cooking and preserve the bright color.

4. Melt butter in sauté pan and add the well-drained broccoli. Season with salt and pepper to taste and toss gently. Arrange on heated serving platter.

Tart Applesauce

2 tart cooking apples, peeled, cored, and quartered
1 cup unsweetened apple cider or juice
Zest of 1 lemon
1 teaspoon honey (optional)

1. Place all ingredients in small, heavy-bottomed saucepan and cook over medium heat 8 to 10 minutes, or until apples are tender.

2. Purée apple mixture in food processor or mash with fork. To serve warm, return to saucepan and reheat over low heat or serve at room temperature.

ADDED TOUCH

A rich upside-down cake, baked in a cast-iron skillet, is a satisfying dessert for this meal. If fresh Bing cherries are not in season, use frozen or canned whole cherries.

Pineapple Upside-Down Cake

5 tablespoons plus 1 stick unsalted butter
⅔ cup brown sugar, light or dark
6 fresh, or canned, unsweetened pineapple rings, drained
1 tablespoon rum (optional)
9 fresh pitted cherries
½ cup plus ⅓ cup all-purpose flour
¼ teaspoon salt
1½ teaspoons baking powder
1 cup granulated sugar
2 eggs
½ teaspoon vanilla extract
⅓ cup milk
Whipped cream (optional)

1. Preheat oven to 350 degrees.

2. Melt 5 tablespoons of the butter in 9-inch cast-iron skillet with ovenproof handle. Tip skillet to coat bottom and sides with melted butter. Sprinkle brown sugar over bottom of skillet. Place pineapple rings on top of sugar and sprinkle with rum. Place cherries in centers and between the rings. Remove from heat.

3. In small bowl, sift together ½ cup of the flour and salt.

4. In another small bowl, sift together remaining ⅓ cup flour and baking powder.

5. In large mixing bowl, beat stick of butter until light and fluffy. Still beating, gradually add granulated sugar, eggs, one at a time, and vanilla.

6. Continuing to beat, alternately add flour and salt mixture and milk. Finally, add flour and baking powder, and mix just until incorporated.

7. Pour batter carefully into skillet and, using a spatula, spread it gently out to the edges.

8. Bake cake in middle of oven 45 to 50 minutes, or until center is springy when lightly pressed with fingertips.

9. Cool in pan on rack 10 minutes, then turn onto serving plate. Serve warm or at room temperature with whipped cream, if desired.

LEFTOVER SUGGESTION

Applesauce, a favorite side dish for pork and other meats, can be warmed, sweetened, and served with cinnamon and cream for breakfast. Plan to double or triple this recipe to make enough applesauce to serve with another meal or two.

Fresh Asparagus Soup
Rack of Lamb with Fresh Mint Sauce
Tomatoes Stuffed with Herbed Rice

Decorate the rib ends of the rack of lamb with paper frills if you like and use pale china bowls to highlight the asparagus soup.

Beverly Cox describes this menu as a typically American company meal. Asparagus has been a favorite American vegetable since colonial days. When selecting asparagus, look for stalks with compact heads and plump, not shriveled, white ends. To keep asparagus fresh for several days, snap off and discard the very ends of the stalks, stand asparagus upright in a container of water, then refrigerate.

Each rack of lamb consists of six or seven chops, enough to feed two—so for four people, you need two full racks. When you buy them, ask your butcher to cut through the chine bone, which is part of the backbone, to make carving

easier. Also, ask him to "French" the ribs for you, that is, to scrape off all the flesh from the ends of the ribs. When you serve the racks, decorate the rib ends with paper frills, which you can buy in a food specialty shop. For medium rare, the racks roast for 30 minutes, but if you prefer well-done lamb, cook the racks another 15 minutes. To test for doneness, press the thickest part of the roast: the more resistance, the more done the meat is.

WHAT TO DRINK

Asparagus tends to make wines taste sharp, so with the

89

soup, omit wine or serve a well-chilled, simple white wine. Rack of lamb, however, needs a good red wine. First choice would be a good Bordeaux from either St. Julien or St. Estephe or a California Cabernet or Merlot.

SHOPPING LIST AND STAPLES

2 racks of lamb (1¾ to 2 pounds each), well trimmed, with
    rib bones Frenched
2 pounds fresh asparagus
4 medium-size ripe, firm tomatoes
2 Spanish onions
1 small bunch fresh parsley
1 bunch watercress (optional)
1 small bunch fresh mint
4 cloves garlic
½ pint heavy cream
3 tablespoons plus 2 teaspoons unsalted butter
¼ pound Parmesan or Romano cheese
4 cups chicken stock, preferably homemade (see page 12),
    or canned
2 tablespoons olive or safflower oil
¼ cup red wine vinegar
⅓ cup rice
1 tablespoon sugar
1 teaspoon dried rosemary, or 2 teaspoons minced fresh
2 teaspoons dried thyme, or 1 tablespoon minced fresh
¾ teaspoon curry powder
Salt and freshly ground pepper
Paper chop frills (optional)

UTENSILS

Food processor or blender
Medium-size skillet
2 medium-size saucepans with covers
Small saucepan
Shallow roasting pan
Shallow baking dish or pie plate
Cooling rack or plate
Small bowl
Colander
Conical sieve or large metal strainer
Measuring cups and spoons
Chef's knife
Paring knife
Carving knife and fork
Metal spoon
Wooden spatula
Whisk
Cheese grater (optional)

START-TO-FINISH STEPS

1. Mince garlic, parsley, and fresh herbs, if using, and follow rack of lamb recipe steps 1 through 4.
2. Follow asparagus soup recipe steps 1 and 2. Chop onions for soup.

3. Chop onions, grate cheese, mince parsley, and follow stuffed tomatoes recipe steps 1 through 3.
4. Follow rack of lamb recipe step 5.
5. Follow asparagus soup recipe steps 3 and 4. Wipe out skillet used for sautéing onions.
6. While soup is simmering, follow stuffed tomatoes recipe steps 4 through 6.
7. Remove lamb from oven, step 6, follow asparagus soup recipe steps 5 and 6, and serve soup while lamb is resting.
8. Five minutes before serving lamb, follow steps 7 and 8, and serve with the stuffed tomatoes.

RECIPES

Fresh Asparagus Soup

2 pounds fresh asparagus
4 cups chicken stock
1½ tablespoons unsalted butter
1½ cups chopped onion
¾ teaspoon curry powder
2 teaspoons salt
Freshly ground pepper
2 tablespoons heavy cream

1. Cut asparagus spears into 1-inch pieces, discarding woody bottoms.
2. In medium-size saucepan, bring chicken stock to a boil.
3. In medium-size skillet, melt butter and add chopped onions and curry powder. Cook over moderate heat, stirring occasionally, until onion is soft but not colored, about 3 minutes.
4. Add asparagus and onion mixture to the boiling stock and stir in salt. Simmer, partly covered, 10 minutes, or until asparagus is tender.
5. Purée soup in food processor or blender, then press through conical sieve or metal strainer back into the saucepan to remove any fibers and attain a creamy texture. If you prefer coarsely textured soup, you may omit sieving.
6. Season with pepper to taste and whisk in cream. Serve hot or chilled.

Rack of Lamb with Fresh Mint Sauce

¼ cup minced parsley
4 teaspoons minced garlic
2 teaspoons dried thyme, or 1 tablespoon minced fresh
1 teaspoon dried rosemary, or 2 teaspoons minced fresh
2 tablespoons olive or safflower oil
2 racks of lamb (1¾ to 2 pounds each), well trimmed, with
    rib bones Frenched
Salt and freshly ground pepper
¼ cup red wine vinegar
1 tablespoon sugar
2 tablespoons minced fresh mint leaves
1 bunch watercress, well washed, for garnish (optional)
Paper chop frills (optional)

1. Preheat oven to 425 degrees.

2. Combine parsley, garlic, thyme, rosemary, and oil in small bowl and spread evenly over racks of lamb. Sprinkle lightly with salt and pepper.

3. Stand racks up in roasting pan, fat side out, and interlace ribs. Cover ends of ribs with aluminum foil to hold racks in place and to keep ribs from charring.

4. Cook in middle of oven about 30 minutes for medium-rare lamb.

5. While lamb is cooking, bring vinegar to a boil in small saucepan. Add sugar and stir until dissolved. Then stir in mint and allow to steep 15 to 20 minutes.

6. When lamb is done, remove it to a serving platter and cover loosely with foil to keep warm. Let stand 10 minutes before carving.

7. Using paper towels or metal spoon, skim as much fat as possible from the pan juices. Add the mint and vinegar mixture to the pan juices and boil briefly, scraping sides and bottom of pan to incorporate any brown bits. Add any juice that has collected around the lamb to the pan and adjust seasonings.

8. Remove foil and cover ends of ribs with paper frills, if desired. Surround lamb with stuffed tomatoes and garnish with bunches of watercress, if desired. Serve mint sauce separately.

To carve: cut between first two ribs on one side. Then cut off rib on other side. Continue to alternate sides, so that rack remains standing until all ribs are carved.

Tomatoes Stuffed with Herbed Rice

4 medium-size ripe, firm tomatoes
1 teaspoon salt
⅓ cup rice
1½ tablespoons plus 2 teaspoons unsalted butter
½ cup chopped onion
2 tablespoons plus 2 teaspoons grated Parmesan or Romano cheese
Salt and freshly ground pepper
2 tablespoons minced parsley

1. Cut a ¼-inch slice from stem end of each tomato. Squeeze tomatoes gently to seed them. Carefully remove and reserve pulp, leaving a ½-inch-thick shell. Turn tomato shells upside down on rack or plate lined with paper towels to drain.

2. In covered medium-size saucepan, bring 2 cups of water to a boil. Preheat oven to 425 degrees. Butter baking dish or pie plate.

3. Dice reserved tomato pulp. Add salt to the boiling water and stir in rice. Boil, partly covered, 5 to 7 minutes.

4. While rice is boiling, melt 1½ tablespoons butter in medium-size skillet and add onion. Cook over moderate heat, stirring occasionally, until onion is soft but not colored, about 3 minutes.

5. Add drained rice to the onion and stir in the diced tomato pulp and 2 tablespoons of the grated cheese. Season to taste with salt and pepper.

6. Place tomato shells in lightly buttered baking dish or pie plate and fill them with rice mixture. Dot with remain-

ing butter and sprinkle with remaining cheese. Bake 15 to 20 minutes. Sprinkle with parsley before serving.

ADDED TOUCH

Fresh strawberries and rhubarb make a delicious filling for this deep-dish pie. Pie is best served warm. You can make it in advance and reheat it; or, you can have the ingredients ready to assemble, so that you can put the pie in the oven to bake while you enjoy the rest of the meal.

Deep-Dish Strawberry Rhubarb Pie

The pastry crust:

1¼ cups all-purpose flour
¼ teaspoon salt
1 teaspoon sugar
½ cup chilled vegetable shortening
3 tablespoons water

The filling:

3 cups fresh strawberries, sliced
2½ cups fresh rhubarb, unpeeled if young and tender, cut into ½-inch pieces
1¾ to 2 cups sugar, depending on sweetness of rhubarb
¾ teaspoon cinnamon
¼ teaspoon freshly grated nutmeg
3 tablespoons flour
3 tablespoons unsalted butter, cut into small pieces
1 egg, lightly beaten
1 egg, lightly beaten with 1 tablespoon of water
Vanilla ice cream or whipped cream (optional)

1. In food processor fitted with metal blade, combine all ingredients for crust and process until mixture forms a ball and pulls away from sides of bowl. Wrap ball of dough in wax paper and chill about 30 minutes.

2. Preheat oven to 400 degrees.

3. Combine strawberries and rhubarb in large mixing bowl. Mix together sugar, cinnamon, nutmeg, and flour, and sprinkle over the fruit. Toss gently to blend; add butter and 1 beaten egg, and toss again.

4. Transfer mixture to well-buttered, deep 9-inch pie dish.

5. On lightly floured board, roll out chilled dough into a circle about 11 inches in diameter. Cut 1-inch-wide band of dough from outside of circle. Brush edge of pie dish with cold water and stick the band of dough around the edge. Brush band lightly with water.

6. Roll remaining dough onto a rolling pin and unroll over dish. Trim and crimp edges so that they adhere to the band of dough.

7. Cut 2 or 3 air vents in crust and use any remaining scraps of dough for making cutouts in the shape of strawberries and leaves.

8. Brush crust lightly with remaining egg beaten with water. Stick cutouts on and lightly brush again. Bake in middle of oven 40 to 45 minutes, or until crust is golden.

9. Serve pie warm in deep dishes with vanilla ice cream or whipped cream, if desired.

Laura Sandifer

L aura Sandifer, an amateur cook who grew up in Atlantic City, New Jersey, comes from a long line of good home cooks. As a Northerner, born and raised, she nevertheless specializes in Southern and soul-food cooking. Her childhood memories focus on her weekly Saturday afternoon cooking lessons, when her mother spent two hours with her in the kitchen. Even now, Laura Sandifer sets Saturday afternoons aside for cooking, no matter how many hours she has cooked and tested recipes during the week.

Today, Laura Sandifer cooks and entertains frequently for her husband and their guests in New York City, where she now lives, and in Sag Harbor, Long Island, where she spends her summers. Guests invariably request one of her Southern or soul-food specialties. The staples of soul food include pork, green vegetables, and dried beans, most of which require lengthy preparation. Laura Sandifer has altered her soul-food recipes here, as with the simmered cabbage and fried pork chops of Menu 2, to accommodate cooks in a hurry. The calf's liver of Menu 1 she describes as Southern style because the meat is served with a gravy.

Green pea soup, served either hot or cold, introduces the Southern-style calf's liver, the buttered dill noodles, and tossed salad. Informal mats and simple dinnerware are perfect for this casual family dinner.

93

Green Pea Soup
Southern Calf's Liver
Buttered Noodles with Dill / Tossed Salad

For the soup in this menu, Laura Sandifer purées cooked frozen green peas, then enriches the purée with sour cream, egg yolk, and butter. You can serve the soup hot and garnish it with croutons and sour cream, as in this version. For homemade croutons, the cook suggests removing the crusts from three slices of white bread, then cubing the slices. In a heavy skillet, heat a half stick of butter until it browns. Sprinkle in seasoned salt to taste, ½ teaspoon chopped fresh dill, 1 clove crushed garlic, and the bread cubes. Stir the bread cubes until crisp, then drain them on paper towels. You can also serve the soup cold and garnish it with diced boiled ham. Make it several hours before you plan to serve it, to give it time to chill.

Liver is an iron-rich source of protein. Calf's liver is always a delicacy, whether sautéed, broiled, braised, or, as in this recipe, baked with plum tomatoes, herbs, onions, and bacon. Calf's liver is costly, and you may wish to use less expensive lamb, beef, or baby beef liver.

Fresh dill enhances the buttered noodles. Fresh dill is available in most greengrocers all year, but if you cannot find it, use dried dill.

The tossed salad, bright with red cabbage shreds, adds a colorful touch to the meal.

WHAT TO DRINK

This unusual mating of calf's liver with tomatoes can best be accompanied by a light- to medium-bodied red wine: a Beaujolais, a California Merlot, or a good non-Riserva Chianti would be ideal.

SHOPPING LIST AND STAPLES

4 slices calf's liver (about 1½ pounds total weight)
½ pound thick-sliced bacon
¼ pound boiled ham (optional)
3 large onions
1 small head Romaine lettuce
1 small head red-leaf lettuce
1 small red cabbage
Fresh dill sprigs
1 egg
½ pint sour cream
1 stick plus 2 tablespoons unsalted butter
2 cups chicken stock, preferably homemade (see page 12), or canned
1½ cups beef stock
16-ounce can Italian plum tomatoes

10-ounce package frozen peas, or 1½ pounds fresh peas
12 ounces broad egg noodles
3 slices day-old bread (optional)
4 tablespoons sugar
½ cup plus 2 tablespoons flour
¼ cup plus 6 tablespoons vegetable oil
1 tablespoon vinegar
1 teaspoon prepared mustard
2 tablespoons Worcestershire sauce
1 tablespoon dried marjoram
1 bay leaf
Salt and pepper

UTENSILS

Food processor or blender
Stockpot or kettle with cover
Large, heavy-gauge skillet
Shallow casserole with cover
Medium-size saucepan
2 small bowls
Colander
Measuring cups and spoons
Chef's knife
Paring knife
Wooden spoon
Tongs
Salad spinner (optional)

START-TO-FINISH STEPS

1. Follow calf's liver recipe steps 1 through 5.
2. Follow salad recipe steps 1 and 2.
3. Follow pea soup recipe steps 1 and 2. Bake calf's liver, step 6.
4. Bring water to a boil for noodles, step 1, and mince dill.
5. Follow pea soup recipe steps 3 and 4. If making croutons, trim bread crusts and cut slices into ½-inch cubes. Place in shallow baking pan and toast in oven 3 to 5 minutes. Dice ham, if using to garnish soup.
6. Follow soup recipe step 5 and serve.
7. Follow salad recipe step 3.
8. A few minutes before liver is done, cook noodles, steps 2 and 3.
9. Follow salad recipe step 4, liver recipe step 7, and serve all together with the noodles.

Green Pea Soup

2 cups chicken stock
10-ounce package frozen green peas or 2 cups fresh peas
2 tablespoons unsalted butter, at room temperature
2 tablespoons flour
1 egg yolk
½ cup sour cream, plus ¼ cup for garnish (optional)
1 tablespoon sugar
Salt and pepper
3 slices day-old bread for croutons (optional)
½ cup diced boiled ham for garnish (optional)

1. In medium-size saucepan, bring chicken stock to a simmer over medium-high heat. Add peas and cook until soft, about 5 to 7 minutes.
2. Purée peas and stock in food processor or blender. Rinse out saucepan and dry with paper towels.
3. In same pan, melt butter, stir in flour, and cook about 1 minute. Stir in purée, and blend well until smooth. Bring to a boil, stirring constantly.
4. In small mixing bowl, blend together egg yolk and ½ cup of the sour cream, making a thin paste. Add paste to the purée and heat slowly, stirring until smooth and thickened. Add sugar and salt and pepper to taste.
5. Serve hot, garnished with croutons and a dollop of sour cream, if desired. To serve the soup cold, garnish with a sprinkling of the ham, if desired.

Southern Calf's Liver

6 tablespoons vegetable oil
4 slices calf's liver (about 1½ pounds total weight)
½ cup flour
8 thick strips bacon
3 large onions, thinly sliced
16-ounce can Italian plum tomatoes
1½ cups beef stock
3 tablespoons sugar
1 tablespoon dried marjoram
1 bay leaf
2 tablespoons Worcestershire sauce
Salt and pepper

1. Preheat oven to 350 degrees.
2. Heat oil in large, heavy-gauge skillet.
3. With paring knife, remove membrane at edge of each slice of liver. Dust slices with flour and brown them on both sides in the hot oil, turning with tongs. Remove liver, place in shallow casserole, and cover.
4. Pour off all but 2 tablespoons of the oil. Brown bacon and onions. Do not remove bacon and onions, but spoon off the fat from pan, leaving about 4 tablespoons.
5. Add remaining flour to the bacon and onions, stirring well to coat. Add tomatoes in their juice, stock, sugar, marjoram, bay leaf, and Worcestershire sauce. Blend well, taking care not to break the tomatoes, and add salt and pepper to taste. Pour the sauce over the liver and cover.

6. Bake about 30 minutes. Remove bay leaf.
7. Serve liver with some of the sauce, including whole tomatoes, and put remainder in gravy boat to pass separately.

Buttered Noodles with Dill

1 teaspoon salt
12 ounces broad egg noodles
1 stick unsalted butter
2 tablespoons minced fresh dill

1. In large stockpot or kettle, bring 2 quarts of hot water to a boil. Add salt.
2. Pour noodles into the rapidly boiling water and cook until just cooked through. Drain in colander and rinse under hot water.
3. Melt butter in same pot in which noodles cooked. Return the noodles to the pot. Stir to coat with butter and mix in dill. Cover and keep warm until ready to serve.

Tossed Salad

1 small head Romaine lettuce
1 small head red-leaf lettuce
1 small wedge red cabbage
1 teaspoon prepared mustard
1 tablespoon vinegar
Salt and pepper
¼ cup vegetable oil

1. Rinse lettuce thoroughly and dry in salad spinner or pat dry with paper towels. Tear into bite-size pieces.
2. Shred cabbage and combine in salad bowl with the lettuces. Refrigerate.
3. Place mustard, vinegar, and salt and pepper to taste in small bowl. With a fork, beat well and gradually add oil, beating to incorporate.
4. Just before serving, pour dressing over salad and toss.

ADDED TOUCH

This is a simple dessert that can be made early in the day, frozen until firm, and then refrigerated.

Quick Chocolate Mousse

12 ounces semisweet chocolate bits
¾ cup boiling water
8 eggs, separated
1 teaspoon almond extract
Whipped cream (optional)

1. Place chocolate bits and boiling water in blender, and process until combined. Mix in egg yolks and almond extract.
2. In large bowl, beat egg whites with electric hand mixer until firm and fold them into the chocolate mixture. Pour into individual molds or 6-cup soufflé dish. Freeze until firm; then refrigerate until ready to serve. Serve with whipped cream, if desired.

Southern-Fried Pork Chops
Cabbage in Yogurt
Boiled New Potatoes / Baked Tomato Halves

Solid-colored plates set off the browned pork chops, braised cabbage in a yogurt-based sauce, parsley-garnished new potatoes, and baked tomato halves. Use different-colored plates to add a festive touch.

Southerners have for years regarded pork as a staple of their diets. Center-cut pork chops are more expensive than other chops because they have more meat and better flavor. To prevent shrinkage and to ensure uniform cooking, use low to medium heat. The pork is done when the meat in the center turns from pink to creamy white.

Smothered cabbage, which Laura Sandifer describes as a typical soul-food dish, accompanies the pork chops. Unlike more traditional versions, in which the shredded cabbage is simmered slowly in cream and bacon fat, this recipe cooks quickly and is still creamy, but relatively low in fat, because it calls for yogurt.

WHAT TO DRINK

Choose a full-bodied white wine or a light red one for this meal. For a white, try a spicy wine, such as a California or Alsatian Gewürztraminer; for a red, have a California Gamay or a young, fruity Zinfandel.

SHOPPING LIST AND STAPLES

4 center-cut pork chops, each about ¾ inch thick
4 medium-size tomatoes
2-pound head green cabbage
1 green or red bell pepper
8 new potatoes
3 medium-size onions
1 small bunch fresh parsley
1 stick plus 1 tablespoon unsalted butter (approximately)
1 cup plain yogurt
½ cup chicken stock, preferably homemade (see page 12), or canned
¼ cup vegetable oil
½ cup flour
1 tablespoon plus 2 teaspoons sugar
1 teaspoon paprika
¼ teaspoon caraway seeds
¼ teaspoon ground thyme
Salt and pepper
½ cup dry white wine

UTENSILS

Large, heavy-gauge skillet
2 large saucepans, 1 with cover, or 1 large saucepan and Dutch oven with cover
10-inch heatproof glass pie plate

Large serving platter
Flat plate for dredging
Colander
Measuring cups and spoons
Chef's knife
Paring knife
Wooden spoon
Metal tongs
Vegetable peeler (optional)

START-TO-FINISH STEPS

1. Preheat oven to 325 degrees for tomatoes and follow step 1. Chop parsley for tomatoes recipe.
2. Slice onion and seed and slice bell pepper for cabbage recipe.
3. Follow boiled potatoes recipe steps 1 and 2. Chop parsley.
4. Follow tomatoes recipe steps 2 and 3.
5. While tomatoes are baking, follow cabbage recipe steps 1 and 2.
6. Follow pork chops recipe steps 1 and 2.
7. Follow cabbage recipe steps 3 and 4. Serve on dinner plates with the pork chops, tomatoes, and potatoes.

RECIPES

Southern-Fried Pork Chops

4 center-cut pork chops, each about ¾ inch thick
Salt and pepper
½ cup flour
1 teaspoon paprika
¼ cup vegetable oil

1. Mix flour with paprika on flat plate. Sprinkle pork chops with salt and pepper, and dredge in flour mixture. Shake off excess flour.
2. Heat oil in large skillet. Brown chops in the hot oil about 8 to 10 minutes on each side. Drain on paper towels. Remove to large serving platter, cover, and set aside on back of stove until ready to serve.

Cabbage in Yogurt

2-pound head green cabbage
4 tablespoons unsalted butter
3 medium-size onions, thinly sliced
1 green or red bell pepper, seeded and thinly sliced
½ cup chicken stock
½ cup dry white wine
1 tablespoon sugar
1 teaspoon salt
¼ teaspoon caraway seeds
¼ teaspoon ground thyme
1 cup plain yogurt
2 teaspoons chopped parsley

1. With chef's knife, halve, core, and shred enough cabbage to make 6 cups.

2. Melt butter in large saucepan or Dutch oven. Add onion and pepper slices, and cook until limp, stirring occasionally.
3. Add cabbage, chicken stock, wine, sugar, salt, caraway seeds, and thyme, and bring to a boil. Cover tightly and steam over medium heat until cabbage is limp, approximately 7 to 10 minutes. Do not overcook.
4. Add yogurt and parsley, and stir gently to incorporate.

Boiled New Potatoes

8 new potatoes
2 teaspoons salt
2 tablespoons unsalted butter
2 tablespoons chopped parsley

1. Scrub potatoes and, if desired, use a vegetable peeler to peel off thin band of skin around each potato.
2. In large saucepan, cover potatoes with water and add salt. Boil gently about 20 minutes, or until tender.
3. Drain potatoes in colander and melt butter in same pan. Return potatoes to pan and shake to coat them with the butter. Add chopped parsley and shake again to coat the potatoes. Keep warm, covered, until ready to serve.

Baked Tomato Halves

4 medium-size tomatoes
2 teaspoons sugar
4 teaspoons salt
8 pats unsalted butter (approximately 3 tablespoons)
8 teaspoons chopped parsley (approximately 3 tablespoons)

1. Cut tomatoes in half crosswise and place them cut side up in heatproof glass pie plate.
2. Sprinkle ¼ teaspoon sugar and ½ teaspoon salt on each half. Top each half with 1 pat butter and 1 teaspoon parsley.
3. Bake in preheated oven 25 to 30 minutes. The tomatoes should remain fairly firm.

ADDED TOUCH

This tart dessert, made ahead, is a perfect finale.

Apricot Egg Cream

4 ounces dried apricots, chopped
1½ cups plain yogurt
3 egg yolks
2 tablespoons sugar

1. Preheat oven to 350 degrees.
2. Place apricots in small bowl with boiling water to cover. Let soak 10 minutes; drain. Place in bottoms of individual ramekins.
3. Mix remaining ingredients and pour over apricots.
4. Place ramekins in heatproof baking dish and add enough boiling water to come halfway up ramekins.
5. Bake 25 minutes, or until firm. Refrigerate until serving time.

Creamy Corn Soup
Broiled Ham Steaks / Fried Apple Slices
Potatoes, Carrots, and Scallions

A plastic serving tray for each guest is a convenient way to serve the ham steak, soup, apple slices, and the vegetables.

Laura Sandifer's creamy corn soup is seasoned with onions, green pepper, celery, and carrots. During the summer, you can use fresh corn cut from the cob instead of frozen kernels. Buy 5 or 6 ears and, with a sharp knife, cut the kernels off the cobs into a bowl; then, using the back of the knife, scrape out the pulp that is still on the cob.

The broiled ham steak, sprinkled with dry mustard and sugar, then soaked in evaporated milk, is a family recipe. Laura Sandifer's mother maintained that the milk, an unusual marinade, gave the ham a distinctive flavor. Fried apple slices, spiced with cinnamon and lemon juice, are delicious with pork. Choose firm, tart cooking apples that are uniform in size and take care not to overcook them or they will become mushy.

WHAT TO DRINK

The combination of sharp and sweet flavors here rules out any but a simple wine. According to your preference, serve either a well-chilled Soave or a Beaujolais.

SHOPPING LIST AND STAPLES

2 ham steaks with bone (about 1 pound each)
3 strips bacon

4 large potatoes (about 2 pounds total weight)
4 large apples, Granny Smith or Golden Delicious (about 1¾ pounds total weight)
1 pound carrots
1 green pepper
1 large onion
1 small bunch celery
1 bunch scallions
Fresh parsley sprigs (optional)
1 lemon
1 stick plus 4 tablespoons unsalted butter
5½ cups chicken stock, preferably homemade (see page 12), or canned
16-ounce poly-bag frozen corn, or 5 to 6 ears fresh corn
7½-ounce can evaporated milk
4 tablespoons plus 1 teaspoon granulated sugar
4 teaspoons brown sugar
2 tablespoons dry mustard
1 bay leaf
1 tablespoon cinnamon
Salt and pepper

UTENSILS

Food processor or blender
Large skillet
Medium-size skillet
Shallow 13-by-9-inch baking dish
Large saucepan
Medium-size saucepan
Small saucepan
2 small bowls
Colander
Measuring cups and spoons
Chef's knife
Paring knife
Wide spatula
Slotted metal spatula
Wooden spoon
Vegetable peeler
Apple corer

START-TO-FINISH STEPS

1. If using fresh corn for the soup, slice off bottoms of cobs so they will "stand" upright; scrape kernels with sharp knife. Be sure to scrape any liquid and pulp still on the cobs. Set aside.
2. Follow potatoes and carrots recipe steps 1 and 2.
3. Follow corn soup recipe step 1.
4. While bacon is cooking, prepare ham, steps 1 and 2.
5. Prepare vegetables for soup: peel and chop onion, dice celery, seed and dice pepper, scrape and dice carrots. Follow corn soup recipe step 2.
6. Preheat oven to 200 degrees. Follow corn soup recipe step 3.
7. Squeeze lemon to measure 2 tablespoons juice and prepare and cook apple slices, steps 1 through 4.
8. Follow potatoes and carrots recipe step 3.
9. Follow ham steaks recipe step 2 and corn soup recipe step 4. Serve.
10. Broil ham steaks, step 3, and follow potatoes and carrots recipe steps 4 and 5. Serve with the fried apple slices.

RECIPES

Creamy Corn Soup

3 strips bacon
1 large onion, coarsely chopped
2 celery stalks, diced
1 green pepper, seeded and diced
16-ounce poly-bag frozen corn, or 5 to 6 ears fresh corn
2 cups chicken stock
2 carrots, scraped and diced
Salt and pepper

1. Fry bacon in medium-size skillet until crisp and drain on paper towels.
2. Add onion, celery, and green pepper, and cook in the bacon fat until limp.
3. If using fresh corn kernels, bring 2 cups water to a boil in small saucepan. Add corn and simmer 5 to 10 minutes. Drain in colander. Or, cook frozen corn according to package directions. Purée corn in food processor or blender. Add the sautéed vegetables to the corn. Stir in chicken stock and carrots, and simmer until carrots are tender, about 5 to 7 minutes. Add salt and pepper to taste.
4. Garnish soup with crumbled bacon.

Broiled Ham Steaks

2 ham steaks with bone (about 1 pound each)
2 tablespoons dry mustard

4 teaspoons brown sugar
7½-ounce can evaporated milk
Parsley sprigs for garnish (optional)

1. Place ham steaks in shallow baking dish. In small bowl, combine mustard and brown sugar, and sprinkle evenly over each steak. Pour evaporated milk over the steaks and set aside until ready to broil.
2. Preheat broiler.
3. Place ham steaks about 5 inches from heat source and broil until brown and bubbly, about 4 minutes. With wide spatula, remove ham steaks to cutting board and slice each in half. Serve on individual plates and garnish with parsley sprigs, if desired.

Fried Apple Slices

4 large apples (about 1¾ pounds total weight)
4 to 8 tablespoons unsalted butter
4 tablespoons granulated sugar
1 tablespoon cinnamon
2 tablespoons lemon juice

1. Peel and core apples. Slice them crosswise into ½-inch-thick circles.
2. In large skillet, heat 2 to 3 tablespoons of the butter, but do not let it brown.
3. Combine sugar and cinnamon in small bowl. Dip apple slices in the sugar to coat both sides. In the skillet over medium heat, brown them in batches, turning them with a slotted spatula and sprinkling with lemon juice as they cook.
4. After each batch has cooked, pour off any juice that has accumulated in the pan; it will keep the apples from browning. Remove cooked apple slices to heatproof platter, cover, and keep warm in oven. Repeat process, adding more butter before cooking each successive batch. Reserve juice and pour over the apple slices when they are all cooked. Remove from oven and cover loosely with foil.

Potatoes, Carrots, and Scallions

4 large potatoes (about 2 pounds total weight)
4 carrots (about ½ pound total weight)
1 bunch scallions
3½ cups chicken stock
1 bay leaf
4 tablespoons unsalted butter
1 teaspoon sugar

1. Peel potatoes and cut into ½-inch dice.
2. Scrape carrots and cut on bias into thin ovals. Trim scallions, coarsely chop, and set aside.
3. Place potatoes and carrots in large saucepan with chicken stock, bay leaf, and butter. Bring to a boil; then reduce heat and simmer gently, uncovered, about 10 minutes, or until vegetables are easily pierced with a fork. Remove bay leaf.
4. Drain vegetables in colander.
5. Turn into serving bowl and toss vegetables with chopped scallions and sugar. Cover and keep warm until ready to serve.

ADDED TOUCH

Chopped walnuts add texture and grated orange peel adds zest to this dense, moist cake—a sweet ending to a hearty meal.

Zucchini Walnut Cake

2 cups all-purpose flour
2 teaspoons baking powder
¾ teaspoon baking soda
1¼ teaspoons cinnamon
½ teaspoon nutmeg
½ teaspoon salt
½ teaspoon allspice
4 eggs
1½ cups sugar
1 cup vegetable oil
1½ teaspoons vanilla
2 teaspoons freshly grated orange peel
1 cup chopped walnuts
1½ cups shredded unpeeled zucchini

1. Preheat oven to 350 degrees. Grease and flour a fluted 9-inch tube pan.
2. Sift flour with baking powder, baking soda, cinnamon, nutmeg, salt, and allspice.
3. In large mixing bowl, beat eggs until light, then beat in sugar until mixture is fluffy. Slowly beat in oil. Blend in the sifted dry ingredients and fold in vanilla, orange peel, walnuts, and zucchini. Spoon into tube pan.
4. Bake 45 minutes to 1 hour, or until a cake tester comes out dry.
5. Cool in pan 15 minutes; then remove to wire rack. Cool completely.

Acknowledgments

The Editors particularly wish to thank the following for their contributions to the conception and production of these books: Ezra Bowen, Judith Brennan, Angelica Cannon, Elizabeth Schneider Colchie, Sally Dorst, Marion Flynn, Lilyan Glusker, Frieda Henry, Jay Jacobs, Pearl Lau, Kim MacArthur, Kay Noble, Elizabeth Noll, Fran Shinagel, Martha Tippin, Ann Topper, Jack Ubaldi, Joan Whitman.

The Editors would also like to thank the following for their courtesy in lending items for photography: *Cover:* cloth and bowl—Museum of American Folk Art Shop; serving platters—Wilton Armetale. *Frontispiece:* baskets—Primitive Artisan, Inc.; quilt and ceramics—Museum of American Folk Art Shop. *Pages 18–19:* mat—Solveig Fernstrom Umbach; napkin—Leacock and Company; silver—Wallace Silversmiths. *Page 22:* flatware and linens—Broadway Panhandler; pottery—Terra Firma Ceramics. *Pages 24–25:* cloth—Sturbridge Village; silver—Wallace Silversmiths. *Pages 28–29:* pottery—Linda Marks from Downtown Potters' Hall; flatware—The Lauffer Company. *Page 32:* table setting—Museum of American Folk Art Shop. *Page 34:* cloth—Fabindia from Primitive Artisan, Inc.; pottery—Claudia Schwide; bowls—Museum of American Folk Art Shop. *Pages 36–37:* cloth—D. Porthault, Inc.; crystal bowl—Orrefors, Inc.; china and crystal—Baccarat; silver—Ercuis Silver. *Page 40:* plate—Arabia of Finland. *Page 43:* china—Buffalo China, Inc.; decanter—Pottery Barn; countertop—Formica Corporation. *Pages 46–47:* cloth—Fabindia from Primitive Artisan, Inc.; glasses—Williams-Sonoma; pottery—Janis Schneider from Downtown Potters' Hall. *Page 50:* enamel plates—New Country Gear; flatware—The Lauffer Company. *Pages 52–53:* cloth—Colonial Candle Gift Shop; serving dishes—Pfaltzgraff Museum of American Folk Art Collection. *Pages 56–57:* cloth, candlestick, and plates—Pierre Deux; rice tureen—Richard Ginori. *Page 60:* pan and casserole—Bazar Français; pottery—Cecily Fortescu. *Page 62:* cloth—Peter Fasano; napkin—Leacock and Company; dishes—Royal Copenhagen Porcelain; vase—The Lauffer Company; glass—Kosta Boda; silver—Wallace Silversmiths. *Pages 64–65:* tableware—Julia Kuttner Antiques; silver—Wallace Silversmiths. *Page 68:* tray and plate—Pottery Barn. *Page 71:* cloth—Calico Cloth; napkin—Leacock and Company; carafe—Pottery Barn; glasses—Baccarat; pottery—Eigen Arts Pottery; flatware—The Lauffer Company. *Pages 74–75:* tiles—Laura Ashley; pitcher—Buffalo China, Inc. *Page 80:* cloth—Mosseri Industries; glasses—Pottery Barn; pottery—Sylvia Finkle and Roxy Weil from Downtown Potters' Hall; flatware—The Lauffer Company. *Pages 82–83:* mats, napkins, and glasses—Pierre Deux; pottery—Barbara Eigen of Eigen Arts Pottery; flatware—The Lauffer Company. *Page 86:* mat—Solveig Fernstrom Umbach; platter—Arabia of Finland; dishes—Pfaltzgraff. *Page 89:* platter—Wilton Armetale; plates—Arabia of Finland; glass and decanter—Colony Glasswear. *Pages 92–93:* mat—Pottery Barn; cloth—Brunschwig and Fils; plates and cutlery—Arabia of Finland. *Page 96:* plates—Pottery Barn. *Page 98:* tray, bowl, and plate—Pottery Barn.
Illustrations by Ray Skibinski.

Index

*Time-Life Books Inc. offers a wide
range of fine recordings, including
a Big Band series. For subscription
information, call 1-800-621-7026, or
write* TIME-LIFE MUSIC, *Time & Life
Building, Chicago, Illinois 60611.*